Words of praise for *Out of Control*

"Ben Young anⁱ a sensi-
tive spot for Arⁱame us
into cutting back on overcommittment and technology dependence,
but leads us into practical, spiritual answers for making sense of our
most precious commodity: our spiritual, emotional and physical
energy. Your kids and your spouse will be glad you read this book."

—DENISE GLENN
Founder of MotherWise Ministries, author of *Wisdom for Mothers*

"If you're too busy to read this book, then this book is especially for
you! Pull up a chair, take a deep breath, and learn how your soul
can be replenished. No speed reading allowed!"

—LEE STROBEL
Author of *The Case for Christ* and *The Case for a Creator*

"This book will change the way you live! I can't imagine anyone
who wouldn't benefit from its practical and grounded advice. Read
it and find the peace you long for."

—LES PARROTT, PH.D.
Seattle Pacific University
Author of *Shoulda Coulda Woulda*

OUT OF CONTROL

FINDING PEACE *for the* PHYSICALLY EXHAUSTED
and SPIRITUALLY STRUNG OUT

BEN YOUNG & DR. SAMUEL ADAMS

NELSON BOOKS
A Division of Thomas Nelson Publishers
Since 1798

www.thomasnelson.com

Published in Nashville, Tennessee, by Thomas Nelson, Inc.

Library of Congress Cataloging-in-Publication Data

Young, Ben.
   Out of control : finding peace for the physically exhausted and spiritually strung out / Ben Young & Samuel Adams.
      p. cm.
   ISBN 0-7852-1193-4 (pbk.)
   1. Peace of mind—Religious aspects—Christianity. 2. Stress (Psychology)—Religious aspects—Christianity. I. Adams, Sam. II. Title.
   BV4908.5.Y68 2006
   248.8'6—dc22

                                                            2005026113

Printed in the United States of America
06 07 08 09 RRD 5 4 3 2 1

CONTENTS

LIVING FREELY AND LIGHTLY

The most peace-filled man who ever lived invited His followers to imitate the simple flow of His life: "Are you tired?" He asked. "Worn out? . . . Get away with me and you'll recover your life. I'll show you how to take a real rest. Walk with me and work with me—watch how I do it. Learn the unforced rhythms of grace . . . Keep company with me and you'll learn to live freely and lightly" (Matthew 11:28–30 THE MESSAGE).

It sounds good, doesn't it? But who has time for "the unforced rhythms of grace" when you can barely cover your list of to-do's? From seniors to boomers, from busters to X-ers, from teens to toddlers (no kidding!), we're players in an overscheduled, over-committed, out-of-control culture. Ours is a high-tech world of instant messaging, speed-dialing, express-lane driving, and multitasking; we're doing anything but living "freely and lightly." Instead, we're addicted to speed, obsessed with work, and overwhelmed by a flood of enabling technology. We want what we want, and we want it now!

Maybe you are a working professional striving to get ahead or simply make ends meet. Perhaps you're one of the many who struggle to maintain the delicate balance between career success and family commitment. Or you might be a parent who feels overwhelmed and

3

overextended as you try to do your best for your children. You may even be a single adult who feels anxious and burdened by excessive pressures and demands from people who believe you have all the spare time in the world. For most of us, our lives have come to resemble a twenty-four-hour convenience store: open for business 365 days a year!

The culture we live in leaves little room for rest and renewal, and the pace of contemporary America is simply not conducive to vital and refreshing spiritual practices. No one gets shout-outs these days for nurturing his or her inner self. We hear talk from time to time about spiritual practices such as solitude, silence, prayer, and meditation, but these things seem to be nothing more than archaic relics reserved for "spiritual giants." Come on—what ordinary man or woman has the time?

We've written this book as a wake-up call for those who feel hopelessly stuck on the treadmill that never stops. We're offering wisdom and practical insight to guide you to the peace and deeper rest you long for.

We think you do. We believe it is possible to slow down and find rest, renewal, and peace in the twenty-first century. We're convinced that you have access to the resources you need to maintain a simpler life: a life of order and freedom at the same time. In other words, you don't have to be out of control. You're not a victim of your culture or your circumstances. Things can change! We've written this book as a wake-up call for those who feel hopelessly stuck on the treadmill that never stops. We're offering wisdom and practical insight to guide you to the peace and deeper rest you long for. We want you to catch a glimpse of another kind of life: one full of joy and peace. And we're not going to ask you to become a monk, a missionary, or a mystic in order to get it.

And in case you're wondering, we're not retired, nor are we living in some ivory tower. We're just like you. We live in bustling cities and have busy families, full professional lives, and various ministry responsibilities. But we've personally tasted the fruit of certain practices that have been around for centuries, and we have found these practices vital to spiritual growth.

We know that nothing takes the place of peace with God and peace of mind. He established the principles of rhythm, rest, and renewal that give real life, and He is ever faithful to keep on providing us with what we need.

If you sincerely desire God's peace—a way of living "freely and lightly"—then put yourself in a position to receive it. Expect God to challenge you through the pages of this book. Pray that He will speak to your heart and prompt you to make the kinds of changes necessary for inner peace and simplicity. Follow Him. We'll do our best to show you how.

ONE

A Culture Spinning Out of Control

Deep-blue Pacific waters sparkle beyond the balcony of your tropical villa. The sun embraces you with its gentle warmth as you sip a frozen strawberry concoction. You have not a care in the world: no nagging pressures, no demands, and no commitments. *This is too good to be true,* you think—and it is. Out of nowhere come the short, insistent blasts of your alarm. It's 6:00 AM! Your blissful dream sinks like a rock. Heart racing and adrenaline surging, you jump to your feet. It's showtime! Go, go, go!

Another hectic day of back-to-back meetings looms, and you're feeling the weight of the day press in. You dress in record time and scarf down a breakfast bar while checking your e-mail, only to be bombarded by thirty-four new messages! In the background, *FOX*

News reporters announce the current homeland terrorist alert level: orange, no less. An update on the latest Middle East bombing follows news of a hijacking in Uzbekistan. It is not yet 7:00 AM, and too much information is flying at you already. When does it stop?

At 7:15 you grab your briefcase and laptop, leap into your SUV, ignoring the running board, and race to the office. The drive downtown is no less hurried and frantic as you zoom down the freeway with a cell phone in one hand and a *venti* Starbucks double-shot, no-foam, extra-hot latte in the other. (Don't all drivers steer with their knees?) Dodging several angry drivers and one near-fatal collision, you exit the urban autobahn and screech to a complete halt at a stoplight.

Aaaah. It's here: the first break of the morning, offering just enough time to download a new message to your Blackberry or glance in the mirror and see to some last-minute grooming issues. Three lights later you're pulling into the parking garage and realizing you've missed *yet another* unscheduled but hoped-for oasis of morning prayer.

Once upon a time, you vowed to start each day with some quiet reflection and solitude because deep down you really *do* desire a simpler life. But as much as you yearn for peace and tranquility, they always elude you. The pressure from every side that comes from trying to hold it all together is unbearably intense. Eventually something's gotta give. Your greatest fear is that if you *did* slow down or let go of even one thing, *everything* would spin completely out of control. Then what? Nervous breakdown? Funny farm? Not this week. You don't have time!

Mommy Madness

Your alarm is always the first to go off—because you're the mommy, that's why. You're up before the sun rises, fumbling around to get yourself together so that you can help your family begin their day well. Multiple wake-up calls rouse the kids, and you assemble and serve some sort of breakfast. Before 8:00 AM you've located several missing socks, made lunches, matched clothes, switched car seats from one car to another, and capped the same tube of toothpaste three times.

Between dropping children off at school and picking them up again, you've executed enough errands to qualify for a spot on *The Amazing Race*. And your day is only half-done! Shuttling to and from ballet class, tutoring, soccer, softball, and play dates requires the logistical savvy of an air traffic controller. You peer over the dashboard of the car with a deer-in-the-headlights gaze as you slowly make your way back home. Then more fun begins: Supper. Baths. Homework. Bedtime rituals. Laundry. Then, across a room crowded with toys, your husband winks at you. Romance? You've got to be kidding. "Not tonight, honey."

> *Supper. Baths. Homework. Bedtime rituals. Laundry. Then, across a room crowded with toys, your husband winks at you. Romance? You've got to be kidding. "Not tonight, honey."*

How do we know what it's like? Because we're married to women who practically do it all—and we've seen what superhuman effort keeping the home ship afloat requires. So whether you work outside or inside the home, whether you have one child or many, if you're a mom, you've experienced your fair share of "mommy madness."

NO PACE, NO PEACE

Question: When was the last time you felt personal peace? Not a kick-back-in-your-chair-with-a-tub-of-ice-cream-and-watch-Oprah kind of mind-numbing nirvana. We're aiming at something much deeper than that: the kind of peace that emanates from the very depths of your soul—a peace that provides substance and satisfaction, as well as a distinct calm in spite of one's circumstances. What price would you be willing to pay for *that* kind of inner peace?

The truth is, you cannot put a price tag on the kind of peace that most of us long for. And it's hard to find physical and spiritual refreshment in a culture that worships activity and discounts the value of rest—especially *soul* rest.

God created this world. He created you and me. He is the Mastermind—the Grand Architect, if you will—and only He knows how we are meant to flourish. It doesn't take a genius to see that God has designed rhythm and pace into the very fabric of His creation. Just look at the cosmos and see the rotation and movement of heavenly bodies, the phases of the moon, the rising and setting of the sun. Here on Earth, observe the distinct cycles and seasons of creation: times of planting and harvest, hibernation and gestation, high tides and low tides. All God's creation moves with the undeniable rhythm of stop and go, ebb and flow, fast and slow.

As humans we are the very apex of God's created order, and our bodies themselves are alive with rhythm. Our hearts beat and our blood flows; even our breathing reflects this inner reality of constant fluctuation. We were designed for times of action and times of rest, but it's tough to keep them balanced in a culture that applauds—even demands—perpetual hustle and bustle. In *Keeping in Step with the Spirit*, J. I. Packer wrote:

> The pace and preoccupations of urbanized, mechanized, collectivized, secularized modern life are such that any sort of inner life is very hard to maintain . . . [and] is difficult

in a world that runs you off your feet and will not let you slow down.

And if you attempt it, you will certainly seem eccentric to your peers, for nowadays, involvement in a stream of programmed activities is decidedly "in" and the older ideal of a contemplative life is just as decidedly "out."

THE SO-CALLED REWARDS OF AN OUT-OF-CONTROL LIFE

Unless you've been living in the outer regions of Siberia, you will certainly relate to the concept of *information and choice overload.* You know all too well the overwhelming feeling that a list of growing responsibilities and 24/7 connectivity can produce. Sadly, we've come to the point where this kind of busy, out-of-control lifestyle is normal. But why is that?

APPROVAL

Society applauds the fast-trackers. Being busy is a cultural status symbol of sorts—even our friends encourage it! Let's face it: to be busy, or at least to appear this way, is to be important. Awards (real and imagined) are bestowed based upon our willingness to overextend ourselves with volunteer activities, extra time at work, and meaningful involvement in the community. We receive bonuses, praise from peers, and the self-satisfaction of being dubbed Selfless Man/Woman of the Year (a bit ironic, isn't it?). Implicit (or sometimes explicit) affirmation often comes to those consumed by their responsibilities.

I recently overheard a group of businessmen at my local coffeehouse affirming their buddy, who was boasting that he put in over seventy hours at work each week, leaving every morning at 5:30 AM, then staggering home at 7:00 PM just in time to tuck his kids in bed. "How do you do it? Where do you get the drive? Way to go— you're the man!" they exclaimed. These men reserved their enthusiastic words of affirmation for a guy who was burning the candle at both ends and who almost certainly was on the way to a domestic or career flameout. Maybe he ain't the man!

SELF-WORTH

The pressure to overextend also comes from within. Our own personal drives and expectations can keep us on the move. Deep needs for self-worth and approval may fuel our crazy compulsion to do more and more, promising a feeling of fulfillment and accomplishment. After all, to be busy *is* to be important, right? This belief is based on the false assumption that more is always better and that external productivity takes precedence over everything, even internal growth. Of course, we don't often realize that this assumption is false, and we just keep plugging away, telling ourselves that to be busy is to have purpose.

SPIRITUAL SIGNIFICANCE

The drive for approval or self-worth provides enough pressure, but some of us get slapped with the ultimate guilt trip: "You've just gotta do more for God!" The church offers great programs, important classes, and enlightening seminars as well as numerous worthy ministries to support, but how much more can one person do? I can remember, early on in my spiritual journey, buying into the notion that religious involvement automatically provided spiritual nourishment and personal growth. I wish I could go back in time and spend an hour in prayer for every hour I spent listening to a boring tape on the "seven steps to effective prayer" or what have you. I would love the chance to go back and get my hands dirty helping out my neighbor in need rather than attending that "life-changing" seminar on the good Samaritan! And I would give practically anything to revisit my first year of marriage and build a stronger relationship with my new bride instead of volunteering hours upon hours of premarital counseling at the church. Being overinvolved is dangerously close to being hypocritical.

When churches place too much emphasis on rules and responsibilities, not near enough time remains for relationship and rest. How can the church be truly countercultural if it is as consumed as the world is with activities? Playing the same game of busyness under the guise of "spirituality" offers little refuge from the inevitable storms and chaos of life. Remember, the church should offer hope and renewal, not contribute to exhaustion and fatigue.

The so-called rewards of an out-of-control life are easy to buy in to, but no matter what, the end result is the same: you and I end up feeling defeated, physically exhausted, spiritually unfulfilled, and disillusioned.

ON THE VERGE OF INSANITY

Our society seems obsessed with productivity and consumption, as well as the accumulation of more wealth and more toys, to the extent that it verges on insanity. Author Richard Foster noted that our contemporary culture blindly accepts the notion that "more is better" without question. He even went so far as to suggest, "The lust for affluence in contemporary society has become psychotic:

it has completely lost touch with reality." We would wholeheartedly agree for many reasons, among which is the fact that the pursuit of more money and material possessions is insatiable. The desire for more becomes a compulsive pursuit with no end. Authors John Degraaf, David Wann, and Thomas Naylor cynically refer to this as "Affluenza," which they define as "a painful, contagious, socially transmitted condition of overload, debt, anxiety, and waste resulting from the dogged pursuit of more." Sounds like they hit the nail on the head.

INSANITY IN THE WORLD AT LARGE

Each of us operates within the larger context of global trends and developments, a good many of them disturbing. Just pick up any Sunday paper and check out the week-in-review section to get an overview of the devastation of civil strife, war, and famine, not to mention the quieter effects of family dysfunction, hypertension, mental illness, AIDS, and STDs.

But that's not all. The news fails to report the apathy that exists toward spiritual things, and the steady decline toward depravity seen not only in our nation but also across the globe. Today we see, rather than a new day of unity, harmony, and world peace, the opposite: more unrest in our homeland, continued discord in the Middle East, animosity toward America, and persistent terrorist threats. All of this can't help but contribute to our growing sense of angst, helplessness, and powerlessness.

INSANITY, COURTESY OF MOTHER NATURE

Even the weather seems to be careening out of control. Natural disasters strike intermittently and have done so since the world began—nothing is new about this. But more floods, more earth-quakes and tsunamis, more hurricanes and tropical storms are occurring today (or at least are more widely reported) than ever before. As the frequency and intensity of these natural disasters come to our attention, the notion that you and I have absolutely no control over our environment is more solidly reinforced! Subtly but surely, these natural threats penetrate our psyches, leading to an overall sense of agitation and fear.

THREE-RING INSANITY

Remember the Ringling Brothers and Barnum and Bailey Circus? The combined chaos of daring animal acts, high-wire stunts, and performances by jugglers and clowns exhilarates to the point of being overwhelming. Add to the visual stimulation of lights, colors, costumes, and movement a curious auditory mixture of animal noises, music, applause, and laughter, and it becomes impossible to take it all in. The typical circus experience features three rings, each with its own separate performance. You might have elephants danc-ing in one ring, tigers jumping through flaming hoops in another, and motorcycle stunts in the third ring.

Sound familiar? We thought so. We see three main rings of influence in this out-of-control circus we call *life*. Let's take a look at each of them.

RING #1: INFORMATION AND CHOICE OVERLOAD

Technological progress is great, but there is a downside to all these hi-fi, wi-fi advances. Simply put, we have too much coming at us from all directions. From *Dr. Phil* to *The O'Reilly Factor*, from celebrities selling Gap jeans to race car drivers hawking Viagra, and from breaking news of another suicide bomber to the latest global catastrophe, we're *drowning* in data.

That doesn't even take into account the work memos, fiscal reports, personal correspondence, and junk mail we must manage. This is the Information Age, and we've got plenty of ways to gather more and more of it—just no help in filtering what comes our way. Simply to stay abreast we must sift through information ranging from the utterly serious and extraordinary to the purely trivial and sensational.

> *From Dr. Phil to The O'Reilly Factor, from celebrities selling Gap jeans to race car drivers hawking Viagra, and from breaking news of another suicide bomber to the latest global catastrophe, we're* drowning *in data.*

For example, do we really need to be reminded that it is below freezing in Fargo, North Dakota, or that another middle-aged actress is having Botox injections? Could any harm come from *not* knowing that lime-green head scarves are in fashion, or that Britney Spears is rumored to be expecting? (By the time this book is printed, I'm sure *People* will have a ten-page spread of the whole family.) Even grocery shopping overloads the consumer with too many options when the average supermarket has tens of thousands of items to choose from! Fifteen varieties of bread, forty-five brands of cereal, and twenty-seven kinds of toothpaste can turn a quick errand into an hour-long excursion.

There is nothing evil or immoral about all this information and all these choices—they're just unnecessary. And they create more mental clutter, confusion, and noise for us to contend with when we have enough already.

RING #2: ACCESSIBILITY OVERLOAD

Many of us are overextended personally and professionally because we allow ourselves to be too accessible. If people can reach us any time of the day or night by cell phone, pager, IM, Blackberry, or fax machine, is it any wonder that they do? And whether we want to talk to them or not, we must spend valuable time checking their messages and deciding how to appropriately respond. Then consider the barrage of junk e-mail that we must delete just so we can get to the things that matter!

> *The real issue here is one of people-pleasing. We are too afraid to hurt others' feelings or let them down, mostly because we want to be liked— so we do more and more and enjoy it less and less.*

While these modern devices are exciting and beneficial, they also represent an intrusion of sorts. This technology has led to a decline in personal space and a deterioration of self-preserving individual boundaries. An unspoken expectation exists that we have to respond to everyone's call and should do so immediately. I don't give out my e-mail address, and people are absolutely incredulous about this. Even random strangers feel entitled to my personal information and e-mail account. What's up with that? When I buy batteries at the Radio Shack, the clerk wants my telephone number, address, social security number, and stock portfolio. And for some reason we feel compelled to dole out every bit of information to the teenager behind the cash register wearing the name tag; then we complain when someone steals our identity.

You wouldn't leave the doors and windows of your home open all day with no say-so about who comes and goes, would you? But we live in a virtual house that's accessible 24/7 to nearly anyone at all, and we wonder why we have no peace!

RING #3: RESPONSIBILITY OVERLOAD

Finally we have the ring of responsibility overload, distinguished by a general posture of overcommitment. Stretched to the max, we still attempt to cram in even more. We seem to have abandoned common sense and have lost the art of pacing our lives. This compulsive drive to do more and more leaves little room for rest, relaxation, or renewal. As a general rule, those suffering from responsibility overload have trouble simply saying no.

One more urgent program, important meeting, significant function, or "necessary" social engagement always comes up, and we seldom refuse any of them. We justify and rationalize many of these commitments in the name of obligation, but, of course, the real issue here is one of people-pleasing. We are too afraid to hurt others' feelings or let them down, mostly because we want to be liked—so we do more and more and enjoy it less and less.

John 5:44 is especially convicting here: "How can you believe when you accept glory from one another and do not seek the glory that comes from the one who alone is God?" (NRSV). What is this glory-seeking John condemns? It's the kind of "glory" that leaves you feeling unfulfilled and tired because it's impossible to please *everyone*, nor should you try. The notion that you *can* please everyone (let alone whether or not you *should*) is an illusion.

EVERY CIRCUS HAS A RINGMASTER

Every circus has a ringmaster, right? The three-ring, out-of-control circus has one too. Though most people mock or ignore his existence, our enemy is alive and active, and he has many of us right where he wants us: busy and preoccupied, scattered and overwhelmed.

The Adversary is happy for you and me to be absorbed with details, focused on nonessentials, distracted by noise, entertained by trivia, frightened by world affairs, and mesmerized by mass media. It's no wonder our kids have ADD! Is it possible that the rival of holy God could be sitting around the boardroom of Hades, smoking cigars and laughing at us for making his job so easy? In times past, I suspect he and his minions had to work much harder with all manners of temptations and seductions in order to persuade and entice men. Now, I'm afraid his strategy is fairly simple: "Just keep 'em busy and distracted!"

Scripture makes it clear that Satan is the prince of this world (1 John 5:19 informs us that the whole world is under the control of the evil one). He directs and controls many of its goings-on. In this

> *If you are the type who needs permission to slow down, then take your cue from Christ. Cut back your responsibilities and minimize your commitments in the name of Jesus.*

sense, he is the ringmaster in this circus of life, directing our attention here and there, broadcasting steady propaganda, orchestrating sideshow entertainments, offering amusing attractions, and creating more noise—all this in an attempt to distract us from the true essentials of life.

But wouldn't it be nice to have a break from the onslaught of draining distractions? Can you imagine a life that moves toward simplicity and away from all these relentless pressures and demands? Would you dare give yourself permission to be less wired, less "responsible," and less accessible to anyone and everyone? If you're looking for permission, how about taking it from the ultimate authority?

Jesus in the Twenty-First Century?

What if Jesus had been born in our day? Judging with our twenty-first-century standards, would we consider His thirty-three years successful ones? Devotional writer Oswald Chambers analyzed Christ's pace of life and concluded that if the amount of service or work (busyness) is the test for success as a Christian, then Jesus Christ was the greatest failure that ever lived. He's got a point! While Jesus was obviously an intentional individual, no evidence exists of a hurried or frantic lifestyle. Instead, the Gospels present a man who was calm, cool, and collected. Where do you ever see Jesus in a screaming hurry?

Can you imagine Him stressing out about His daily agenda? "Let's see, I've got a budget meeting with Judas at seven, followed by an exorcism at nine, and then a nine-thirty anger management session with Peter. Oh no! I have twelve healings to conduct before close of business today. When will I ever have time to confront the hypocrisy of the Pharisees and still manage to hear all the prayers that are lifted up in My name?"

Instead, consider how many times Jesus withdrew from His busy world to be alone with the disciples, or with the Father. We see Christ regularly retreating to the wilderness, away from the noise, the crowds, and the rush of life—an incredibly convicting fact! Matthew 14:23 tells us that He went by Himself up to the mountains to pray, and when night fell, He was still alone. If Jesus Christ, the second person of the Trinity, needed that time alone, how much more do we? Or consider Luke 5:15–16, which reminds us again that because of the crowds of people pressing in on Him, Jesus slipped away to a lonely place and prayed.

The Son of God left some people unhealed and others hungry or even demon possessed. He was apparently not consumed with doing more and more, and He certainly didn't load up His schedule with a lot of programs, events, and committees. On the contrary, Jesus waited until age thirty (some today would say almost past His prime) to settle into His true "career." Even so, He had plenty of time to do His Father's will: He needed only three-and-a-half years!

If you are the type who needs permission to slow down, then take your cue from Christ. Cut back your responsibilities and minimize your commitments in the name of Jesus. Some of you may cynically retort, "Well, Jesus lived in an undeveloped, agrarian society, and He didn't have to deal with the stresses and hassles that we face today." Granted, He did indeed live in a slower-paced culture, but He faced emotional barriers and enormous stresses far beyond what you and I will ever encounter. These included daily pursuit from people who craved His attention, His touch, His "magic"—not to mention the conspiracies to kill Him and plots to thwart His mission. On top of all that, He experienced intense spiritual warfare and direct, full-on encounters with Satan himself. I'd say the cultural differences are a wash in light of these facts.

THE MISSING PEACE

Peace and simplicity won't "just happen" to you. Not in this life. You cannot continue to go with the flow of our culture, adopt its attitudes and priorities, and expect to have inner peace. Consider what Thomas Merton said: "To surrender to too many demands, to commit oneself to too many projects, to want to help everyone in everything is to succumb to violence. Frenzy destroys our inner capacity for peace." In other words, you cannot maintain the pace of our culture, give in to all its expectations and responsibilities, and still know peace.

No one is immune to the stresses and challenges of contemporary life, not even Christians. Yes, we are empowered with God's Spirit, equipped with His Word, and upheld by His promises. But even so, we will no doubt experience struggles. That's just life! We don't get to skip the rough spots, but in the midst of them it is possible to know peace, security, comfort, and safety. Just look at a few of these encouraging promises:

- We have freedom now, because Christ made us free. (Galatians 5:1 NCV)

- I will hear what God the LORD will speak, For He will speak peace To His people and to His saints. (Psalm 85:8 NKJV)

- Now may the God of hope fill you with all joy and peace in believing . . . (Romans 15:13 NKJV)

Those of us who know Christ know that He is the answer . . . and that the promises of God are not empty. Deep down we do believe—but how do we claim and appropriate what God has made available to us? How do we escape the out-of-control, three-ring circus and find true peace and rest?

PUTTING IT IN PERSPECTIVE

It's time to put all this in perspective. In spite of the fact that our culture fosters an out-of-control lifestyle, we do have choices.

We are not locked into a lifetime of stress and chaos. Believe it or not, hope and blessing await those who are willing to follow God's principles for rest and renewal. As impossible as it may seem to you right now, you can walk away from the treadmill and significantly slow down the pace. Many already have.

This is a book about learning to live a very different life and learning to make radical changes in the way you manage and organize your time here on earth. With this guide, we believe you will discover a peace that passes all understanding, find the power to overcome the worries of this world, and develop the perspective to transcend the distractions of your life. And when you've begun to consistently do these things, we suspect you will want to pass them on, especially to the people you love.

What If . . .

. . . you gave yourself permission to slow down and reflect on the madness of this fast-paced culture?

. . . you allowed yourself to believe that a life filled with peace is truly available to you?

. . . you asked God to speak deeply to your heart as you search for insights concerning rest and spiritual renewal?

TWO

ARE *YOU* OUT OF CONTROL?

You can observe a lot by seeing.
—YOGI BERRA

James came to see me for counseling purely at the request of his wife. He claimed to have no idea why she might have suggested it. Oh, sure, he admitted, he snapped at the kids every once in a while and watched a lot of television in the evenings. But that was just his way of unwinding after a busy day at the office. Business was good, he said, and income was steady, although he was spending nearly every waking moment at work. James loved his wife but felt she was being overly sensitive about their problems. All in all, he considered their lives pretty good—or at least as good as those of most of their friends.

Meanwhile, across town, James's wife, Karen, was telling a high-powered divorce attorney that she was at the end of her rope.

She simply could not live another day with a man who was "completely detached from me and the children," obsessed with work, and, when he was home, "oblivious" to anything but the drone of the television or the sirenlike lure of the Internet.

James and Karen weren't just on opposite sides of town that day; they were living in two completely separate realities. Does it surprise you that an intelligent, successful, well-intentioned man like James could operate under the illusion that everything in his life was fine while wreaking havoc and creating disappointment for the people around him? It shouldn't. We see it all the time.

Sadly, we could cite case after case of men (and women) like James who just didn't see disaster coming or couldn't recognize the warning signs of an out-of-control life. Like him, these individuals usually seek help after (or on the verge of) a nasty wake-up call; and those wake-up calls can come in many forms. James's call was a relational one. But serious illnesses, nervous breakdowns, forced unemployment, or addictions can be the red alert that something *must* change.

Tragically, many are so busy or distracted in the pursuit of their version of the American dream that they don't realize what a nightmare their quest has become. As one sage has put it, "The only way to get out of a nightmare is to wake up." But we're suggesting that it may be possible to *wise up* before receiving a nasty *wake-up* call you don't want to answer! While many of us have a vague sense that something's not quite right, most of us don't know how to distinguish between normal stress and the experience of being out of control (OOC).

HEEDING THE WARNING SIGNS

The way to change before a rude awakening blindsides you is to examine the warning signs in your life. Plato said, "The unexamined life is not worth living." We're not suggesting that the oblivious, unaware person has nothing to live for, but we *do* believe that self-examination is a means to discovery. If you desire a life of purpose, peace, and clarity rather than one of complacency, just getting by, or quiet desperation, it's time to wise up and heed the warning signs.

We're used to warning signs. That little "check engine" light on your car dashboard is one, and it's probably one that you heed. No one relishes the thought of being stranded on the side of a busy freeway or interstate, hoping to be delivered by another motorist's random act of kindness. When the dashboard light comes on, we take action—or we should.

I remember a time when I did not respond as I should have to the "check engine" light, and I paid a price for it. When I first saw the warning, I was too distracted and preoccupied with other important tasks to take my car in, and after a few days of seeing the light's tiny glow with no apparent consequences, I began to ignore it altogether. Over time, the indicator faded to the background, and I wasn't even aware of it anymore. What once meant "warning" had simply become normal. I was reminded of it later, though, when my car broke down on a hunting trip deep in south Texas, miles from civilization. Suddenly, things weren't so normal anymore.

Over time, the frantic pace we keep in our out-of-control lives

> *To our detriment, we're all quite advanced in the art of image management.*

becomes so familiar that it feels normal too. Besides, most of the people we know are just as stressed out as we are and seem to be managing fairly well. But the truth is, many of them are not managing well at all—they're just managing to keep up appearances. To our detriment, we're all quite advanced in the art of image management.

So the question is, do you want a life that simply *looks* well managed and under control, or one that truly *is* peaceful, purposeful, and well lived? If the latter sounds more attractive to you, perhaps you're ready to wise up to the warning symptoms that, on their own or in combination, precede almost every wicked wake-up call.

Here they are. Consider them carefully. Your future really does depend on how honestly you are able to examine your own life.

- Out of Shape
- Out of Sorts
- Out of Touch
- Out of Time
- Out of Focus
- Out of Balance
- Out of Order

ARE YOU OUT OF SHAPE?
(PHYSICAL SYMPTOMS)

The most obvious signs of the out-of-control life are physical ones. When you are under stress, your body will let you know it. Problems with sleep and low energy, along with feelings of exhaustion, will begin to manifest. In fact, according to the National Sleep Foundation, nearly one-third of Americans sleep less than seven hours per night, and one in five is so sleepy during the day that his daily activities are hindered.

Whether or not you're getting enough sleep, you may also experience certain body ailments, aches, and pains. Persistent headaches, backaches, and general muscle tension can be warning signs. Other more serious symptoms may be evident too, including chest pain, high blood pressure, gastrointestinal distress, and more.

If you require excessive amounts of stimulants like coffee and other high-energy drinks to keep you on the move, you may have a problem. The latest research suggests that caffeine is fine in moderation, but our culture has a distorted view of *moderation.* Consuming three or more cups of coffee per day is actually considered excessive from a medical standpoint. (A note to those who may be in caffeinated denial: one double-shot latte or cappuccino contains about as much caffeine as three cups of regular brewed coffee. If that's your morning Starbucks routine, you're done for the day! [*National Geographic,* January 2005])

Conversely, when your attempts to wind down at night require the overuse of over-the-counter sleep aids, prescription drugs, or alcohol, you've got a problem.

More literally speaking, the out-of-shape person is one who fails to exercise on a regular basis. In our book, this is a stand-alone warning sign, whether you have

> *A note to those who may be in caffeinated denial: one double-shot latte or cappuccino contains about as much caffeine as three cups of regular brewed coffee. If that's your morning Starbucks routine, you're done for the day!*
>
> —National Geographic, *January 2005*

other physical symptoms or not. At the top of everyone's list of reasons not to exercise is always, "I just don't have time; I'm too busy." This is a wonderful excuse. The president of the United States will put the entire world on hold to pause for exercise and maintain physical fitness. If he has time, certainly you do too.

Listen, anyone who does not regard the need to make aerobic

exercise (heart rate elevated for just twenty minutes or more) a part of his or her life is OOC, period. Walking, running, biking, swimming, and the like *must* be a part of your routine to maintain a healthy lifestyle. The benefits of exercise are simply too numerous to mention, but here are a few: it relieves stress, helps increase heart and lung capacity, tones muscles, helps reduce physical pain, and activates mood-enhancing endorphins. Need we say more?

So then, how about you? How are you doing in the physical realm? Are you out of shape?

ARE YOU OUT OF SORTS?
(EMOTIONAL/MENTAL SYMPTOMS)

Emotional and mental symptoms may be more difficult to recognize than physical ones, but they, too, contribute to an out-of-control lifestyle. Common complaints of the emotionally out-of-sorts man or woman include nonspecific, persistent feelings of anger, irritability, and agitation that can manifest as slight impatience and frustration or in outright anger. (Anyone who's observed road rage has seen this phenomenon.) Or perhaps as a spouse or parent, you completely lose it with your partner or the kids.

Out-of-sorts people may also have trouble relaxing due to obsessive thoughts, worries, and ruminations. They may have difficulty concentrating as well. For example, they might seem fuzzy-headed, scattered, or easily distracted: a form of society-induced ADHD that has no Ritalin fix.

Those who tend to dismiss these emotional and mental symptoms as trivial, take note: unchecked out-of-sorts symptoms can (and often do) spiral into more serious problems such as clinical depression, anxiety, or panic attacks. If you suspect this is true in your case, or if your symptoms significantly interfere with your daily functioning, do yourself a favor and consult your physician for an assessment. It's not weak—it's smart.

ARE YOU OUT OF TOUCH?
(RELATIONAL SYMPTOMS)

Those who are out of touch are relationally disconnected and reserve little time for intimate relationships. For the out-of-touch person, family and friends routinely take a backseat to other, "more important" agendas.

The typical American household has so many technological toys and gadgets that it may become a challenge to connect even with those in your own nuclear family! For instance, it is not uncommon to find a dad checking his stock portfolio in his home office while his teenager is upstairs on the Internet, IM-ing a friend; Mom is on the phone with a neighbor; and the younger children are watching videos in their own rooms. If we're not careful, we can become plugged in to everyone and everything but the people who matter most.

> *No matter what the latest business efficiency best seller says, it is impossible to maintain a relationship with someone without spending* quantity *time with him or her.*

No matter what the latest business efficiency best seller says, it is impossible to maintain a relationship with someone without spending *quantity* time with him or her. Being present in body but absent in mind or heart simply doesn't count. Anyone whose fast-paced life interferes with the establishment and maintenance of meaningful relationships is in danger of becoming out of touch. Is this you?

ARE YOU OUT OF TIME?
(SCHEDULING SYMPTOMS)

Another classic symptom of the out-of-control life is related to the use of time. Out-of-time people frequently complain that there are not enough hours in the day or moan repeatedly about their jam-packed calendars. All of us wish for an extra hour or two on some days, but out-of-time people are ruled by their schedules. They tend to be chronically late to social engagements and business meetings; they double book themselves on purpose to try and do more in less time.

These individuals often rush from one agenda item to the next. They speed up when the traffic light turns yellow and roll through stop signs with hardly a tap on the brake. They're the ones thumbing their Blackberrys in the elevator on the way up to the office and multitasking manically in airports and waiting rooms.

Our culture seems to reward the out-of-time person. Americans work more hours per day for more days per week than workers of any other industrialized nation. We even work more than the medieval peasants did! We also take less vacation time than any other nation. The Japanese are guaranteed twenty-five vacation days each year by law, and the European Union mandates that same number. Americans on average will take ten vacation days each year—and that's after working three years for the same company!—according to the *Austin American Statesman*, September 5, 2004 (quoting William Dietrich of the *Seattle Times*).

Is this you?

New Orleans Public Library

Alvar Branch
913 Alvar Street
New Orleans, LA 70112
504-596-2667

Date: 1/10/2019 Time: 12:31:52 PM

Name: PICUS-FAVRE, MARK JORDAN

Fines/Fees Owed: $0.00

Items checked out this session: 2

Title: God's story, your story : when His becomes yours
Barcode: R0028171370
Due Date: 01/31/2019 23:59:59

Title: Out of control : finding peace for the physically exhausted and spiritually strung out
Barcode: R0020103933
Due Date: 01/31/2019 23:59:59

ARE YOU OUT OF FOCUS?
(PERSPECTIVE SYMPTOMS)

This is perhaps the least obvious of all the symptoms, but it's no less significant than the rest. Out-of-focus people tend to live vicariously through others. They fail to get a handle on their own lives because they are hyperfocused on the lives of others.

This could be a dad who signs little Johnny up for football and baseball during the same season whether Johnny wants to play or not; he may even hire a personal coach or trainer for eighty-five dollars an hour during the off-season. This dad is also at every practice, game, and workout, giving the sense that he has no life beyond his child's next ball game.

Moms can exhibit out-of-focus behavior as well, rushing their children from one activity to the next as if their very lives depended on the crunch of appointments, from soccer practice to piano lessons after school, to tutoring and youth group activities at night. In this kind of child-centered family, *the kids run the show* and life revolves around them: a very dangerous message to send to a preadolescent or adolescent child.

Moms, dads, remember: the very best thing you can do for your children is have a solid marriage relationship with your partner, as well as a full, passionate life of your own. If you're living through your children, you're out of focus.

Men and women can manifest out-of-focus behavior when they become consumed with the personal lives of celebrities to the detriment of their real relationships. Several years ago I had to confront my wife because she seemed to know more about Brad Pitt's personal life than she knew about me. She knew his diet and weight, workout routine, latest romantic interest, next haircut appointment, and upcoming vacation plans. Thanks to *In Style* and *People* magazines, *Entertainment Tonight* and other "news" shows, she had become an unwitting student of Mr. Pitt—not a thing conducive to our relationship!

Both men and women can exhibit this same symptom through a fixation with sports or sports figures. Out-of-focus people are not old-fashioned, sports-on-the-weekend fans. They're the people listening to sports radio on the way to work, having sports-related debates during the day, checking stats on the Internet several times a day, and heckling the players when they attend a game! This kind of misplaced focus is almost always accompanied by the avoidance of personal responsibilities and of opportunities for reflection and growth.

In short, it's impossible to live your own life well when you're preoccupied with someone else's, no matter who that someone is. What about you? Are you out of focus in this way?

Are You Out of Balance?
(Interpersonal Symptoms)

Out-of-balance people do everything for others and leave little or no time for themselves. Many kind and well-meaning people get wrapped up in the ones they love and lose sight of their own needs, but this is not a healthy way to live.

Christians often share a common misconception that carving out significant time for self is selfish and wrong, but a quick read of any of the four Gospels will show that Jesus Himself did this! It is easy to get overwhelmed in the constant push to minister, teach, serve, sacrifice, and work for the kingdom and for others without taking the individual time necessary to recharge, reflect, and restore.

Another symptom of the out-of-balance life is an obsession with control. Clinically speaking, the behavior of control freaks is sometimes referred to as "codependent": attempting to control other people and circumstances in order to compensate for one's own inner turmoil. Codependents feel so out of control on the inside that they look for needy or dysfunctional people to fix so that they themselves can maintain the illusion of control. (More on this illusion later!) The attempts of an out-of-balance person to fix, heal, change, manipulate, or otherwise manage others' lives can be a wonderful way to avoid their own stuff and feel better about themselves.

ARE YOU OUT OF ORDER?
(SPIRITUAL SYMPTOMS)

Misplaced eternal priorities is perhaps the most significant and dangerous symptom of the out-of-control life. Each of us is a spirit being who, for now, resides in a physical body. God designed us for relationship with Him, and only He is able to quench our deepest thirst. To be spiritually out of order is to neglect this vital connection with God.

> *We practice the tyranny of the urgent when we too often focus on important things—not on eternal ones. When your eternal priorities are out of order, you will almost surely miss out on God's best design for your life.*

If you don't start your days with prayer and reflection in order to get grounded in what matters most, you may have your priorities out of order. If you don't have the time to engage in those endeavors that will have lasting impact, you may be suffering from symptoms of spiritual neglect. We practice the tyranny of the urgent when we too often focus on important things—not on eternal ones.

When your eternal priorities are out of order, you will almost surely miss out on God's best design for your life. You see, God created each of us in His image, with a unique purpose to fulfill. Detached from God, a man or woman has no direction or guidance toward that destiny or purpose. Further, disconnection with God causes disconnection from the spiritual resources and power we need to accomplish our divine purposes!

Again we ask, what about you? Are you tapped in spiritually? Do you know how to rest in His presence? Do you know who you were meant to be, and are you living out that purpose for which you were created?

IT'S ALL CONNECTED

Imagine that you are driving your car along the freeway, and all at once, several (not just the check engine light) of the warning lights on your dashboard light up. Would you suspect something serious and head for the next exit or continue to drive and hope for the best? We're guessing you'd pull over. There's something a little more alarming about seeing several lights than in seeing just one, isn't there?

Maybe this chapter has shown you that you have several symptoms of an out-of-control life; very likely it has, because many of these symptoms are interrelated and feed off of one another.

In much the same way, the reverse is true. When we are able to bring one area of life under control, it becomes easier to address others as well. What we're after here is not to pound you for "failing" the test. Instead, it's to open your eyes to the possibilities of a full, free, and abundant life, the kind of life Jesus talked about when He said, "I came so they can have real and eternal life, more and better life than they ever dreamed of" (John 10:10 THE MESSAGE).

We want to show you that it's not just the absence of negatives that can make our lives richer and fuller, but a deliberate cultivation of positives. A world of difference exists between not feeling bad and really feeling good. To put it another way, wouldn't it be nice to begin thriving rather than merely surviving? When our lives are out of control we can easily convince ourselves that all we want is to alleviate some pain and stress, but we'd like to suggest to you that there's more—much more—to it than that.

C. S. Lewis articulated it best when he said, "We are half-hearted creatures, fooling about with drink and sex and ambition when infinite joy is offered us, like an ignorant child who wants to go on making mud pies in a slum because he cannot imagine what is meant by the offer of a holiday at the sea. We are far too easily pleased."

Now, about control. Writing a book called *Out of Control* seems to imply that we can, by ourselves, regain and maintain control. To some degree we can. But complete control is an illusion. It's God's jurisdiction, not ours. We can do some things to make sure we experience the "more and better life" Jesus spoke of, but there are others we cannot control. We can't control nature, sickness, or other people's hearts. We can't control terrorism, cancer, or crime. Ultimately, we cannot control any of the events, circumstances, or relationships associated with our lives.

What we do have enormous influence over is our own hearts, and that is where much of our battle takes place. And because our hearts can fool us sometimes, we're going to ask you to do two more things before we move on. First, give the list of out-of-control symptoms you just reviewed to someone who knows you well and loves you, and ask how *he or she* thinks you're doing. Then, take the self-inventory at the end of this chapter, being as honest with yourself as you can about where you stand. When you're done, we'll be ready to look at seven false beliefs that can keep us stuck in out-of-control mode. We think you'll recognize many, if not all of them. Why? Because we did too.

OOC Self-Inventory

The following list of symptoms should help you decide whether your life is out of control. Be honest with yourself as you consider the symptoms in the checklist below. Place an X in the space next to each symptom you experience, then total your responses.

___Regular complaints of feeling tired

___Fatigue or exhaustion at the end of the day

___Excessive need for energy drinks or more than two cups of coffee/tea

___Significant changes in sleeping patterns: too much or too little

___Tension headaches

___Digestive problems

___Difficulty with appetite

___People telling you that you look tired

___No regular exercise routine

___Irritability

___Chronic anxiety

___Excessive worry

___Agitation

___Difficulty with concentration and attention

___Impatience

___Cynical or negative attitude about life

___Isolated, loner

___Disengaged from others

___Disconnected from family

___No time for meaningful social interaction

___No intimate relationships

___More than ten hours/week of television viewing

___Excessive use of video and computer games

___Overwhelmed

___No regular quiet time with God

___No full day of rest in a given week

___No time invested in meaning and purpose

___Living in survival mode

___Accused of being a workaholic

___Feelings of helplessness

___Inability to say no

Total: _____

How many responses could you identify? What pattern of symptoms do you display? Sometimes it is helpful to see in black and white. If you put a mark by one to four symptoms, you may be in extreme denial. If you scored over twenty-five, book the next flight to Tahiti, and don't forget to bring this book along with you.

Please note: if this combination of symptoms significantly interferes with your functioning, please consult a trusted physician to assess for clinical anxiety or depression.

What If . . .

. . . you asked God to order your days in a way that was truly productive?

. . . you started being proactive about getting into physical shape?

. . . you were fully present in the relationships that matter most?

THREE

Seven Lies That Feed the OOC Lifestyle

It was a beautiful letdown the day I knew
All the riches this world had to offer me would never do.
—Jon Foreman, Switchfoot

We think by now you'll agree that, one, we live in a fast-paced culture that produces chaos, and, two, that you may have a little something to do with feeding that out-of-control (OOC) lifestyle yourself. Perhaps you identified with some of the warning signs we introduced in Chapter 2 and are even convicted about their seriousness. You know you need to change. If this were a typical self-help book, right about now we'd be offering you five easy steps to peace, or a thirty-day stress "detox" program guaranteed to make you mellow.

But we're not going to, because this is not a typical self-help book. In fact, we believe that people cannot help themselves out of the messes they're in and find true peace and rest on their own. But be assured that help exists. We're going to offer some suggestions. (We promised our publisher we would.) But before we ask you to change what you *do*, we're going to ask you to change how you *think*. Chances are good that you may have begun this process already simply by having picked up this book.

It has long been established that behavior and emotions follow thinking. In other words, our lives tend to move in the direction of our most dominant thoughts. One of the wisest men who ever lived concurred, saying, "For as [a man] thinks in his heart, so is he" (Proverbs 23:7 NKJV). Our thoughts are so powerful that the value of right thinking cannot be overstated. It is virtually impossible to think wrong and live right.

So before we change our behavior, we're going to have to change any misdirected thinking—conscious or unconscious—that we may be doing. Let's look at seven cultural lies that form our deepest assumptions and affect the attitudes of our hearts and, therefore, our actions.

We should tell you now that in our view, we can sum up the benchmark for right thinking in the teachings of one man, Jesus Christ. Simply put, Jesus Christ was the most significant and influential human being to grace the planet, period. We mark our calendars based on His birth. His life has driven the course of history. And His sacrificial death and resurrection have transformed millions upon millions of men and women who believe in Him. He was a compassionate healer, a loyal friend, a brilliant teacher, and a radical revolutionary. He presented a whole new paradigm to the religious and political leaders of His day, so much so that some considered Him a dangerous extremist. The wisdom He possessed was out of this world—and it's just the kind of wisdom we need today to counteract the lies and toxic assumptions we choose to believe.

So, let's look at each of the seven lies one by one and see how they stand up in light of the teachings of the only Son of God. (And in case you're one of those people who tends to skip past the preliminaries and cut to the chase, a word of warning: don't. These truths are foundational, and unless you get this, nothing else in later chapters will make sense. Think first, remember? Then do.)

LIE #1: TRUE PEACE IS ONLY FOR MONKS AND MYSTICS

Long ago there lived a man named Frank. Young Frank was born into a family of wealth and social distinction, but he was never really comfortable in his life of privilege. One day while attending church in his little village, Frank felt God calling him to a new kind of life. He walked to the town square, and, in the presence of his wealthy father, stripped himself naked and left everything behind to embrace a life of poverty, celibacy, and simplicity. Maybe you know Frank by his formal name: Saint Francis of Assisi.

A lot of us wrongly believe that we can attain true peace and simplicity only through radical self-denial, á la Saint Francis, and that the only escape from the chaos and clamor of our culture is to abandon it completely. But Christ never said that. He said, "Peace I leave with you, My peace I give to you" (John 14:27 NKJV), not "Peace I leave with you if you sign up for full-time missions work," or "Peace I leave with you if you denounce every worldly asset and leave your clothes in a heap, then head for the Umbrian hills." You get the drift, right?

When Jesus said these words, He was speaking to His disciples just a short time before His death, resurrection, and ascension into heaven. They weren't going to be leaving this world—He was. He wasn't telling them how to escape their culture; He was telling them that they needed His peace to survive *in* it. And so do we. We don't have to check out to get God's peace. He offers it right now, in whatever circumstance we may find ourselves.

The fact is, true peace is less about our circumstances or surroundings than it is about our internal reality. The peace that Jesus Christ gives is solid, sure, and accessible even to ordinary, run-of-the-mill "saints" like us. It's His peace. And He gives it to us when we are rightly related to Him.

One of the great lies of the Deceiver is that we aren't entitled to receive God's blessings unless we are "super Christians." Even some of us who know Jesus well and follow hard after Him get caught up in this one. But it's not about a spiritual hierarchy. Paul wrote in Romans, "Therefore, having been justified by faith, we have peace with God through our Lord Jesus Christ" (5:1 NKJV). We not only have peace *with* God through His Spirit residing in us, but we have the capacity to experience the peace *of* God, even if our names are not Francis or Billy Graham.

Some believe true peace is only for monks and mystics, but the truth is, unlimited peace is available to all of us through Jesus Christ right now, right where we are.

Lie #2: To Achieve Success in the Eyes of the World Is to Be Significant

Most of us were taught at an early age that the way to gain significance is by amassing a solid record of worldly achievements and accomplishments. So we work hard at what the world values, measuring our lives and our worth by our performance against someone else's standard. The math is simple: more work plus more progress equals more applause and, therefore, more significance. We learn to take pride in activity, even if it's not activity we enjoy. If the world thinks it's important, we're ready to prove we can excel at it!

Sometimes, however, our natural desires and giftedness don't match the world's picture of success. Take John, for example. He proved himself to be a creative and gifted artist as an adolescent, but his father quickly let him know that art was not a reasonable calling or vocation. He said it was, at best, only a hobby—and not a very masculine one at that. His father would have much preferred that John excel in sports, and he labeled his artistic son a "misfit" and a "loser."

John didn't know that he already had worth as a human being created in the image of God. So in order to please his dad and to feel significant, John went to college and majored in business. Then he worked hard to succeed in the corporate world, climbing his way up the ladder, receiving accolade after accolade. After many years and a tremendous amount of effort, he finally won the approval of his father and the community at large. There was only one problem: John was miserable. He wasn't a businessman at heart, and he knew it.

On the eve of his thirtieth birthday, John realized that no one had ever affirmed him for who he was. He suddenly understood, for the first time, he was significant because he was a child of God. If only he had recognized this valuable truth, he could have pursued his dream as an artist. His passion was still art. He was a painter, not a hard-charging executive, in his soul. What a tragic realization after so much striving! The good news is that it wasn't too late for John to take hold of his dream. With his newfound knowledge of God's specific love for him, he felt free to pursue his passion in spite of what anybody else may have thought.

The Bible teaches that God loves and values us as His unique children not for anything we've done, but because of who we are. Jesus said, "Look at the birds of the air, for they neither sow nor reap nor gather into barns; yet your heavenly Father feeds them. Are you not of more value than they? . . . But seek first the kingdom of God and His righteousness, and all these things shall be added to you" (Matthew 6:26, 33 NKJV).

Did you hear that? Just *being* gives us worth in God's eyes. We have inherent value because God created us in His image and we are part of His family. This value is constant and complete. It is not something we can accrue more and more of based on our activity or achievement. Our performance, our possessions, even our personalities cannot change our true significance, which is based on the unchanging character of God Himself. Every morning before my kids leave for school, I (Sam) gently exhort them, saying: "Don't forget who you are!" This worth in God's eyes is so foundational that I will continue to stress it no matter how redundant it may seem to them.

Some believe that to achieve worldly success is to be significant, but the truth is, we already have infinite worth as children of God.

LIE #3: IT'S UP TO US TO FILL OURSELVES

Did you know that you have a hole in your soul? Each of us has a deep and infinite longing within that the things of this world cannot fill. We try, of course. But even when we're managing to "win" the rat race, we still notice a gnawing hunger for something more. We can get possessions, relationships, titles, awards, and applause and still feel empty. That's because the hole we're trying to fill is not shaped like any of those things. It's shaped like God.

What philosopher Blaise Pascal called our "God-shaped vacuum" is meant to be filled by the infinite God Himself, not with any finite substitute. So no matter what we're stuffing into our emptiness, if it's not God, it's not working.

Whether we acknowledge it or not, our deepest desire is for relationship with our Creator. He made us that way. Only He can meet our hunger for meaning. Jesus said, "I am the bread of life. He who comes to Me shall never hunger, and he who believes in Me shall never thirst" (John 6:35 NKJV). He claimed to be *the* solution to the hunger we can't satisfy!

We don't take in the Bread of Life by knowing about Him or by waving at Him once a week in church. Perhaps this sounds weird, but bear with us. We take Him in, and He fills our deepest desires when we nurture our relationship by spending time with Him. The longer we ignore this relationship or try to put something else in its place (money, relationships, food, sex, alcohol, and so on), the longer we hunger and thirst. There's just no way around it.

> *What philosopher Blaise Pascal called our "God-shaped vacuum" is meant to be filled by the infinite God Himself, not with any finite substitute. So no matter what we're stuffing into our emptiness, if it's not God, it's not working.*

Personally speaking, when I begin each morning with a sacred appointment with God and nurture that connection throughout the day, I approach life from the standpoint of being fulfilled rather than empty and grasping. When I am rooted and grounded in Him, I experience my best days because *the pressure is off*! I don't have to prove anything or justify my existence; I am free to really live because I'm not preoccupied with seemingly noble tasks, superficial relationships, and senseless pleasures in an effort to find satisfaction.

Some believe that it's up to us to fill ourselves, but the truth is, only a daily relationship with God can fill our deepest needs.

LIE #4: WHAT WE IGNORE CAN'T HURT US

Life is difficult. The speed at which it passes by offers us some distraction from this harsh reality, but it cannot mask the fact altogether. Life routinely presents a series of problems to be solved and losses to grieve. It is filled with suffering, hurts, and disappointments that we cannot afford to ignore or deny.

In his book *The Road Less Traveled,* Scott Peck wrote, "Our tendency to avoid problems and the emotional suffering inherent in them is the primary basis of all human mental illness." In other words, we ignore the difficulties of life at our own peril. Instead, Peck said we should face our problems head-on and be intentional about addressing them.

If your doctor alerts you to a suspicious lump, your avoidance may result in tragic consequences. If your child displays severe hyperactivity and attention problems and you choose to ignore it, you may experience significant repercussions down the road. If you max out three credit cards and yet continue to apply for new ones, you are driving on the road to never-ending debt. Our willful ignorance of problems brings and worsens consequences.

Still, many times we maintain a busy and preoccupied lifestyle, thinking it is a convenient way to avoid life's difficulties. As strange as it may sound, the willingness to boldly accept the truth that life *is* difficult is the very thing that allows us to transcend its difficulties! And until we accept this, no matter what we use to distract us—even acts of benevolence—will only leave us stunted spiritually and emotionally. This is a case where ignorance most certainly is *not* bliss.

Some believe that ignorance is bliss, but the truth is, when we face life honestly and directly, we are able to transcend its difficulties.

Lie #5: Resting Is Lazy and Unproductive

One of the classic misunderstandings associated with rest is that it tends to encourage passivity or sloth. Nothing could be further from the truth. True productivity *requires* periods of rest. If you doubt the wisdom of this statement, consider nature. God designed man in such a way that he requires regular times of care and feeding. We take breaks during our day to eat so that our bodies can have fuel. We sleep regularly to heal and restore the body to its peak operating standard. Resting isn't lazy; it's necessary and wise.

Not only is rest good for the body, it nourishes the soul and spirit too. As we slow down, our souls can be refreshed and energized, enabling us to focus anew on the things that matter most. In their book *The Power of Full Engagement,* Jim Loehr and Tony Schwartz argue that the management of energy, not time, is the fundamental currency of high performance. Professional athletes know this and build rest into even the most rigorous training regimens. Busy executives do it too. Their capacity to fully engage tasks, people, projects, and deadlines depends on the ability to periodically *dis*engage.

What about President George W. Bush? He regularly takes time out for leisure, not because he is lazy or bored, but because he knows that without it he is less equipped to face the demands and challenges of being the leader of the free world.

When we balance energy expenditure with energy renewal,

we are even more energized, more fully engaged, more effective, and more productive in our endeavors. Even though it seems counterproductive, to withdraw from the rush and responsibility of life is exactly what we need to be equipped for those responsibilities.

Is it any surprise that Jesus knew this? He regularly disengaged from the demands of His earthly ministry to be alone and rest and to spend time in the presence of His heavenly Father. He made no apologies for it. He actively pursued that time, and He taught His disciples likewise: "Take My yoke upon you and learn from Me, for I am gentle and lowly in heart, and you will find rest for your souls" (Matthew 11:29 NKJV). Jesus invited those who would follow Him to find rest in Him. He called this process of learning to rest a "yoke" because He realized it would take effort for them to pull away from the demands of their culture. It takes no less effort today; in fact, some might argue it takes much more. In any case, the results are the same: a fuller, more stable, and productive life.

Some believe that resting is lazy and unproductive, but the truth is, rest enhances productivity.

LIE #6: WE'RE GOING TO LIVE FOREVER

Perhaps the most intriguing of all the lies that keep us running on the fast track is this one: *I'm going to live forever.* We hate to be the ones to break the news, but *you are going to die.* That's right, you. Oh, we all know this intellectually, but most of us live (for as long as we're able) as if this little truth applies to everyone *but* ourselves.

Os Guinness, in *The Long Journey Home*, said: "Modern society itself is one grand diversion—the republic of entertainment. With our shops, shows, sports, games, tourism, recreation, cosmetics, plastic surgery, virtual reality, and the endless glorification of health and youth, our culture is a vast conspiracy to make us forget our transience and mortality." We deny the inevitable.

We stumbled upon a Web site recently called Deathclock.com, which invites you to provide your birthdate, some medical information, and gender. In return, you will receive the "exact" date of your death. Of course, this is all based upon insurance actuary tables and is tongue in cheek; nevertheless, it is a little sobering. It chips away at our collective denial and provides a humorous reminder that life is slipping away.

> *Our busyness offers a wonderful diversion to keep us from wrestling with the fact that we are going to die. We don't consciously pursue a busy life as a way to avoid thinking about death, but on some level, that seems to be the way it works.*

"Death," said writer Mike Mason, "is something which builds by slow degrees of awareness like the unfolding of a murder mystery in which we ourselves turn out to be the victim." It's ironic, isn't it, that this most definite of all realities is one of the most frequently denied? It's almost as if there is a universal collusion of sorts to dodge the fact of our mortality. Your family is in on it. So is your doctor. Your employer. Your friends. It's no wonder we act as if we are immortal!

The practical significance of this charade is that our busyness offers a wonderful diversion to keep us from wrestling with the fact that we are going to die. We don't consciously pursue a busy life as a way to avoid thinking about death, but on some level, that seems to be the way it works. Thomas à Kempis wrote in *The Imitation of Christ*, "You should order yourself in all your thoughts and actions as if today you were about to die." He's right.

Jesus had something to say about the kind of man who thinks he's going to live forever:

> The ground of a certain rich man yielded plentifully. And he thought within himself, saying, "What shall I do, since I have no room to store my crops?" So he said, "I will do this: I will pull down my barns and build greater, and there I will store all my crops and my goods. And I will say to my soul, 'Soul, you have many goods laid up for many years; take your ease; eat, drink, and be merry.'" But God said to him, "Fool! This night your soul will be required of you; then whose will those things be which you have provided?" (Luke 12:16–20 NKJV)

Only a foolish man denies the reality of death.

Some believe they are going to live forever, but the truth is, each of us will die . . . and there won't be any making up for lost time in the afterlife.

Lie #7: What We Can Build Is Permanent

Tom knew he was approaching his last days on earth, so he kept reminding his wife, Joanna, what to do with all of his stuff after he passed on. "Honey, be sure to put all my golf clubs, clothes, hunting rifles, deer trophies, and gold coin collection in the attic so I can take them with me on my way up to heaven," he said. Joanna complied with her husband's strange request and placed all of his valuables in the attic.

Shortly thereafter, Tom passed away. They had the funeral, and several days had gone by when Joanna thought about all the stuff she'd put in the attic for dear old Tom. She wondered if he had picked it up. So she pulled open the attic door and carefully made her way up the stairs. When she got to the top and looked around, all of Tom's things were still there! She climbed back down the stairs and muttered to herself, "I knew I should have put his stuff in the basement."

Obviously, that is a humorous story, but it illustrates a serious point. Closely related to the illusion that we will live forever is this notion that whatever we can build here on this earth is permanent and lasting. Let's face it: we devote enormous amounts of energy, time, and resources to acquiring, building, and growing our little kingdoms here on earth. We consume and accumulate more stuff, add more toys, build bigger and better homes, all in the false belief that those things will somehow last, or at least be appreciated and kept by our children and our children's children.

What did Jesus have to say about the things we build on earth? Simply put, He promised that they would not last. He stunned His own followers by clearly stating, "My kingdom is not of this world" (John 18:36 NKJV). They had hoped it was. They had believed it was. He refused to let them linger in that assumption, telling them instead: "Do not lay up for yourselves treasures on earth, where moth and rust destroy and where thieves break in and steal; but lay up for yourselves treasures in heaven, where neither moth nor rust destroys and where thieves do not break in and steal. For where your treasure is, there your heart will be also" (Matthew 6:19–21 NKJV).

We spend so much effort trying to create a cozy little existence here on this earth. We're all about creature comfort, convenience, and status. But the very things we think are ours forever are susceptible to so much more than we realize. Jesus said even seemingly harmless things like moths and rust can destroy our treasures. If that is so, imagine what natural disasters, thieves, or even time itself can do!

Instead of amassing our treasures on this earth and loving the things of the world, Jesus instructed us to set our sights and our affections on another place: heaven. Why? Because it *is* permanent. It is *not* passing away. We are citizens of another kingdom, and we have been given permission to get preoccupied with our true and lasting home. "Seek those things which are above," said the apostle Paul, "where Christ is, sitting at the right hand of God. Set your mind on things above, not on things on the earth. For you died, and your life is hidden with Christ in God" (Colossians 3:1–3 NKJV).

A modern-day poet, Jon Foreman, said it like this:

In a world of bitter pain and doubt,
I was trying so hard to fit in
Until I found out,
I don't belong here

Some believe that what they can build is permanent, but the truth is, this world is passing away, and the true kingdom is yet to come.

THE LUXURY OF THE TRUTH

In John 8:32 Jesus said, "And you shall know the truth, and the truth shall make you free" (NKJV). The truth really *will* set us free. Think about it: each of the seven lies has in common this idea that we *can* make life work. When we realize we cannot, we have the luxury of stepping off the treadmill and beginning a journey that really goes somewhere!

In Christ, we have the freedom to live the simpler life of peace and rest. The pressure is off. We are no longer compelled to relentlessly pursue power, prestige, money, or materialism. We don't have to compensate for the deep longing of the soul; He fills it. We don't have to rely on constant motion to make life meaningful; He makes it meaningful. We don't have to live in denial, be afraid to slow down, or pretend we're immortal and that our self-made kingdoms are unshakable; His truth frees us from all of that.

The most exciting part of all this is that you can adopt this attitude today, right now. You don't have to attend years of counseling; you don't need the clergy's blessing; you don't even need medication to help you get there. It's your choice to believe that what God says is true.

The only question is this: Will you exchange the lies of the world for the truth of God? Are you ready to think differently from the way you've thought before? If you are, *we dare you to move.*

WHAT IF . . .

. . . you lived life as though you were just passing through on your way to your true home?

. . . you dared to exchange the lies of this world for the life-changing truths of God?

. . . you asked God to give you a thirst for the things that will bring you true happiness and fulfillment?

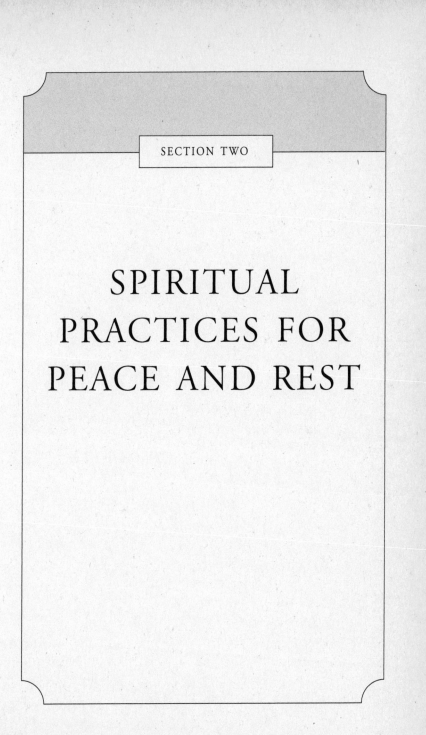

SPIRITUAL PRACTICES FOR PEACE AND REST

We ended our last chapter with a dare: we challenged you to make a move. But we're not suggesting the kind of move you are used to. We're daring you to move from control to mystery; from sustained, chaotic activity to periods of silence and solitude; and from practiced self-reliance to deep faith and trust in God. We're daring you to experience true peace and rest.

So much of the peace and rest we manage to get these days turns out to be nothing more than pathetic attempts to cope with the busy routines of life. For example, vegging out in front of the television, taking a power nap on the weekend, or masking our distress with food and drink wind up offering temporary solutions to deeper problems. These types of mechanisms don't reach down to our souls; by definition, they cannot offer the deeper rest, relief, and renewal that we desperately crave. Even the standard seven-day family vacation turns out to be nothing more than a hectic scramble from one busy activity to another. It's entertaining and loads of fun, but certainly not restful and relaxing in the deeper sense. As Thomas à Kempis once said, "All men desire peace, but few desire the things that make for peace."

So what makes the difference? What will set us up for the kind of rhythm and rest we so desperately long for? What kind of avenues will provide for that truly satiating experience—soul rest and inner peace?

The Hebrew word for "peace" is *shalom*—derived from the word *shalem*—which literally translated means "completion," "wholeness," or "perfection." This idea of wholeness stands in stark contrast to the feelings of fragmentation, distractedness, and turmoil we often experience in our fast-paced world. The kind of peace we're advocating is not simply the absence of chaos, time constraints, or societal demands, but rather an abiding, internal well-being of the heart and soul. That's *shalom*. And that's what we want for you.

> The kind of peace we're advocating is not simply the absence of chaos, time constraints, or societal demands, but rather an abiding, internal well-being of the heart and soul. That's shalom. And that's what we want for you.

This kind of peace is an inside job. We cannot achieve it by pursuing life according to our own agendas. Only God can change our hearts and provide the lasting peace and rest we all desire. Saint Augustine was right when he said, "You stir us to take pleasure in praising You [God], because You have made us for Yourself and our heart is restless until it rests in You." It is our firm belief that a life of peace and rest comes only through a deep, sustained, and intimate relationship with God. Thus, everything we say from here will move toward that end.

We're going to highlight some simple but powerful spiritual disciplines, or practices, that foster the peace and rest we've talked about. These practices, in and of themselves, don't *bring* peace and rest—only God can do that—but they put us in a position to receive it. Remember, we said this is not your typical self-help book, and we mean to make good on that promise. Jesus said in Matthew 16:25, "Anyone who intends to come with me has to let me lead . . . Self-help is no help at all. Self-sacrifice is the way, my way, to finding yourself, your true self" (THE MESSAGE).

Some of these practices may be new to you. Others may not be. Maybe you've heard them called "spiritual disciplines." Whatever term is used, the meaning is the same: these are God-prescribed ways to develop the inner life. Think of them as a core set of exercises to strengthen your inner person much in the same way that physical exercises (and the repetition of them) develop your body. They work. But to discover just how *well* they work, and how good they will make you feel, you'll have to do them—not just learn about them, think about them, or agree with us that they are healthy and life-giving.

And, by the way, it is not wrong to be motivated to practice these disciplines in anticipation of how good they will make you feel. In his book *Journey of Desire*, John Eldredge wrote, "All the Christian disciplines were formulated at one time or another in an attempt to heal desire's waywardness and so, by means of obedience, *bring us home to bliss*" (emphasis ours). Pastor and author John Piper took this a step further by saying that "God is most glorified in us when we are most satisfied in Him." Seeking God for the satisfaction He gives—and then reveling in it—glorifies God just as much as it pleases us. Maybe more.

God is passionate in His desire to demonstrate His authority. We are not in control of our hours and our days. He is. He wants His children to be utterly dependent upon Him; He is out to sabotage our scheming for control because He knows it will not bring us the happiness we desire. So, if your life is out of control and you want peace and rest—if you seek true *shalom*—we dare you to move into abandonment to God and to stop grasping for what you think you lack. Instead, let go of what you know. All deep change and spiritual growth follow a pattern of birth, death, and rebirth. Jesus said, "Unless a grain of wheat falls into the ground and dies, it remains alone; but if it dies, it produces much grain" (John 12:24 NKJV).

This letting go won't be easy. Dorothy Sayers said, "It is always strange and painful to have to change a habit of mind; though when we have made the effort, we may find a great relief, even a sense of adventure and delight, in getting rid of the false and returning to the true."

So what about you? Are you ready to experience true peace and rest? Then let the adventure begin . . .

FOUR

IT ALL STARTS WITH THE SABBATH

"Remember the Sabbath day, to keep it holy. Six days you shall labor and do all your work, but the seventh day is the Sabbath of the LORD your God ... Therefore the LORD blessed the Sabbath day and hallowed it."

—EXODUS 20:8–11 NKJV

I somehow missed it. I had invited Jesus to come into my heart. I read the Bible. I prayed. I was ordained as a minister. I attended seminary. I even spent some time on the mission field. But in spite of all that, I lacked something. Something huge and unnamed dogged me, something I knew I desperately needed. It was identifiable to me only by its gnawing absence.

Then one day, I was invited to appear on a talk show together with a Muslim, a rabbi, and a Buddhist monk. (I know this sounds like the setup for a lame punch line, but bear with me. It's far from that.) The Muslim, the rabbi, the monk, and I discussed several religious issues of the day, but what I remember most about our time together was something the rabbi revealed about his personal life. This man was married with six children and lived in the fourth-largest city of the United States (Houston), yet he and his family managed to consistently practice the Sabbath.

Every Friday evening they shut off their cell phones, computers, televisions, and radios and shared a ritual meal together. I must have appeared incredulous, because he assured me this happened *every* Friday night. "Didn't your kids rebel when you turned off the TV?" I asked. "No," he insisted, "they loved it." *Loved it!*

What he said resonated deeply with me. In fact, it more than resonated: it convicted me. As soon as I heard him talk about setting apart a day to the Lord and refusing to allow anything to disturb that deliberate rest, I knew what I'd been missing. Even though I'd been a Christ-follower my entire life, I had somehow missed the concept and practice of Sabbath rest. The rabbi was experiencing a kind of peace that I didn't have, and I wanted it.

As I reflected on my life and my schedule, I had to admit I had become a slave to the clock and the calendar. I saw rest as an optional luxury and the Sabbath as a slightly archaic Jewish tradition. And while I could easily recall a time when Sundays were more leisurely because fewer businesses were open and blue (morals) laws were in force, I knew that my Sundays (and my family's) were far from peaceful. Like most of my peers, I viewed Sunday as a day to worship, then to catch up on work. Others I knew thought of Sunday as a day to watch football, run a week's worth of errands, sleep off a hangover, or shop 'til they dropped. We've got to stay active, right? God forbid we might actually slow down, reflect, consider our priorities, and ponder our mortality.

Okay. Maybe you *aren't* nursing a hangover or planning your next shopping spree. Maybe you think your priorities aren't that far out of whack. But consider this: When was the last time you devoted an entire day to nothing but prayer, quality time with your family, and rest? When was the last time you cut off every technological tether that keeps you connected, in order to distance yourself from distraction?

I asked those questions of myself after hearing the rabbi speak of the Sabbath. And I'm guessing your answers are probably similar to mine.

Writer Lauren Winner, a convert from Orthodox Judaism to Christianity, says that the aspect of Judaism she misses most as a Christian is practicing the Sabbath: "There is something in the Jewish Sabbath that is absent from most Christian Sundays: a cessation from the rhythm of work and world, a time wholly set apart, and, perhaps above all, a sense that the point of *Shabbat*, the orientation of *Shabbat*, is toward God."

She's right. Christians can be some of the worst about not observing a true Sabbath, or *Shabbat*, as she calls it. But does it have to be so? Could we be missing something important? I believe we are, and perhaps we are missing it because we don't understand what we have lost.

So what is this thing called *Sabbath*, if it's not just a Jewish tradition?

THE STORY BEHIND THE SABBATH

In his excellent book *The Rhythm of Life*, Matthew Kelly said the Sabbath answers our need as human beings for rest: "The seventh day tradition upholds, protects and ensures our legitimate need for rest and relaxation, for a change of pace, for time with family and friends, for time to turn toward the transcendental, and for time to renew our connection with God." Noted Jewish scholar and theologian Abraham J. Heschel called the Sabbath "a day on which we are called upon to share in what is eternal in time, to turn from the results of creation to the mystery of creation; from the world of creation to the creation of the world."

The first thing we need to understand about the Sabbath is that its true Creator was God Himself. And He made the Sabbath for us, not us for it, or it for Him! God doesn't need rest. He never slumbers nor sleeps. The Bible tells us in Genesis that God created the heavens and the earth in six days, and on the seventh day He rested. It's easy to read that account and think: *Boy, God must have been exhausted after He created everything. I know I would be!* But God is not like us. He is altogether different. We are made in His image; He was not made in ours! In other words, He rested to show us that we must also rest. In fact, a Jewish tradition suggests that on the seventh day God continued to create—and what He created was the concept of Sabbath rest!

> *God created us to live from our very first day with eternity clearly in mind. In eternity we will not labor and toil under the sun; we will worship God and live in His light. You and I are made for eternity, not for time!*

It is also interesting to consider that God left the making of man and woman for the sixth day of creation. Have you ever thought about the implications of His creative order? Man was made, then immediately called to rest! Did you catch that? God could have created man earlier in the week so that he could "help." He didn't. God didn't need man's help. He didn't breathe life into Adam and Eve and say, "Okay, team. Get after it. I need to see some activity from you. Knock yourselves out until I say it's time for a day off." He created them, and then He called them to rest. From this order they could understand that they were designed to live from a state of rest, a state of worship, and a state of dependence upon God for everything.

In this sense, God created us to live from our very first day with eternity clearly in mind. In eternity we will not labor and toil under the sun; we will worship God and live in His light. You and I are made for eternity, not for time!

God made no mistake in His divine ordering of creation. He meant to give us rest from the beginning, not as an afterthought. He instructed His people to observe the Sabbath He created because He wanted to bless them with *menuha,* the Hebrew word for "rest." This *menuha* was God's sole creation on the seventh day. He rested on that first Sabbath not because He was tired, but because He was wise and good. He knew that we needed *menuha* not only for our physical, emotional, and psychological well-being, but also in order to strengthen our relationships with Him.

For this reason, we strongly believe that the concept of Sabbath rest is the key to living a life of peace. All the other practices and movements we will discuss in subsequent chapters will flow out of this idea. And by the way, we're not advocating a return to Jewish law-keeping here. We're calling for a commitment to emotional, physical, and spiritual renewal through the observance of a principle that is timeless and true.

Jesus Himself spoke of the Sabbath, not as a set of laws to be kept, but as a concept to embrace. He reminded His disciples when questioned by the Pharisees, "The Sabbath day was made to help people; they were not made to be ruled by the Sabbath day" (Mark 2:27 NCV). And He called them to Himself as the provider of true Sabbath rest. We know we need this rest. Don't you?

The Beauty of the Sabbath

It's entirely likely that at this point you are thinking of the Sabbath as a form of legalism that you needn't bother with, or as a kind of "spiritual spinach" that you might try but almost certainly won't enjoy. What we'd like for you to see, however, is that the practice of the Sabbath has always been quite beautiful—and can still be beautiful today.

I was recently fortunate enough to reconnect with the rabbi I met on the talk show. I spoke with him at length about *Shabbat* and his family's observance of it. I figured something that has endured for three thousand or so years must have more to it than meets the eye, and I was right. Think about it: all the saints of the Old Testament, from Moses to Joshua and all the way from David to Malachi, practiced the Sabbath. It has legs!

Here is what I learned from my friend, the rabbi: An observant Jewish family prepares for *Shabbat* for the entire week. On Friday at sundown, they unplug from culture and reconnect with God, family, and friends. In the days prior to *Shabbat*, the mother has cleaned the house and prepared a three-course meal and a kind of bean soup called *cholent*. A crisp white tablecloth adorns the dining table. Eighteen minutes before the sun sets, she lights candles and places two braided rolls of bread and a bottle of wine at the center of the table. The two rolls symbolize the double portion of manna God gave for the Sabbath to the wandering Israelites. (On every other day, they only received one portion and could not store up extra.)

The traditional Sabbath meal begins with the singing of two songs. One song refers to the choices one makes on the Sabbath: either to squander it or to make it something valuable. The second is a song of gratitude to the one who made the Sabbath preparations (usually the mother of the family). After the family has sung, the father blesses each of his children. He speaks three-sentence blessings over them, based on verses from the books of Numbers and Genesis. He lays his hands on the children's heads and kisses them; then they, in turn, kiss their father and mother.

Next, the father sanctifies the wine, performs a ritual hand-washing, and blesses the bread. Then the family eats the three-course meal (no wonder they sing praise to the mother!) and sings various ancient songs. After the meal is finished, the family retires for the evening.

The next morning, the family walks together to the synagogue, where they hear the Torah (the first five books of the Old Testament) read and prayers offered. They will worship God together with other friends and family from morning until noon, then walk home again. The mother serves the noontime meal she prepared beforehand—usually the *cholent*. The father again blesses the wine and bread, and the family eats. When the meal is done, family members may nap or read (writing is forbidden on the Sabbath). At around 4:30, they will return to the synagogue for more prayers, songs, and instruction from the Torah.

Now, allow this to sink in for a moment: for thirty-three years, Jesus Christ, the beautiful Son of God, experienced the beauty of the Sabbath with His earthly family *in just this way*.

Your Identity in the Sabbath

"That's well and good," you may be saying. "I agree that there is a beauty in the traditional observance of the Sabbath. But that's just not me. First of all, I'm not Jewish, and second, I'm *way* too busy to shut down for an entire day." We hear you. We aren't Jewish (by race) either, and we're fairly busy guys as well. But we believe in the practice of Sabbath rest because in it we've found out more about ourselves than we might have otherwise known. Practicing the Sabbath causes you to face and feel the essence of your humanity. Too often we think we are what we buy or own or do. But in Sabbath rest we are stripped of these defining things. Our props are removed. We are reminded of the limits of our humanity and of God's complete otherness or transcendence.

Suddenly, we're not the toys we play with or the things we use to make life more manageable. (We remember how PDAs, cell phones with Bluetooth, Blackberrys, iPods, and all the other gadgets we love to show off actually complicate our lives!) In Sabbath rest, it's just us . . . and God. And if we're lucky, *then* we're able to see how those things we relied on to define us and make us feel important actually strip us of all that we truly are in Christ.

Once you begin to practice Sabbath rest, you will see that God is the only one who is able to rightly define you. In a good marriage, each person simply enjoys being in the other's presence, period. Their activity is secondary, the place is inconsequential, the trappings are superfluous. In much the same way, the more deeply you delve into your relationship with God, the less reliant on constant stimulation you will become. You simply begin to enjoy His presence, and to enjoy who you are *in* His presence. You are free to worship Him as He is and to be known as you are.

THE POWER OF SABBATH REST

Power and rest aren't usually concepts you think of together. But there *is* power in Sabbath rest, and it exists because of the one who lived, died, and rose on our behalf. While the Jewish Sabbath tradition calls men and women to rest in the sufficiency and provision of God, Christians who practice Sabbath rest do so in the completed redeeming work of the Son of God, Jesus Christ. He is the one who offers eternal rest from man's striving to please a holy God. And it's a good thing He does, because a holy God can never be satisfied with anything but complete holiness. And apart from Christ, you and I will never have it.

Think about it: there is nothing you can do to satisfy God's demand for holiness. You can't work hard enough, pray long enough, or serve unselfishly enough for God to accept you. Your performance, your moral report card, is never going to be good enough for God, because He demands absolute perfection. To meet His standard of righteousness, we would have to perfectly obey every law of His in thought, word, and deed—for life! Even if this were possible, the very nature we inherited from our original dysfunctional family (Adam and Eve) would disqualify us.

This would be very bad news, except for the good news. And the good news is this: Jesus Christ lived a perfect life and died in our place so that we could be reconciled with God. He lived, He worked, He strove for and achieved perfection so that we might be covered for the thousands and thousands of times we have broken God's laws and fallen short. Through the power of the resurrected Christ, you and I can stop posing and striving and hoping to impress God with our inadequate performances and rest in the completed work of Jesus Christ. That is a powerful peace, isn't it?

> *Through the power of the resurrected Christ, you and I can stop posing and striving and hoping to impress God with our inadequate performances and rest in the completed work of Jesus Christ. That is a powerful peace, isn't it?*

Sabbath rest is a weekly reminder of this daily reality. Keeping the Sabbath is a physical practice with profound spiritual realities. Of course, a day of rest restores us physically, emotionally, and psychologically, but it is primarily a wonderful weekly reminder that God has done it all for us and we can rest in His grace and provision.

THE OVERFLOW OF SABBATH LIVING

When we have received the gift of rest in Jesus Christ's perfect sacrifice, we are free to enjoy the overflow of Sabbath living. Every single day we can observe and celebrate the Sabbath by relying on Him and not ourselves. While setting aside one day of the week would be an optimal way to observe the Sabbath, we don't want you to have an all-or-nothing mentality when it comes to Sabbath rest. What we'd like to promote instead is Sabbath *living*.

If one day a week seems reasonable to you, by all means, give it a try. I (Ben) found this concept to be so compelling that my wife and I made a commitment to observe the Sabbath weekly. Each Sunday, my family and I go to church and Sunday school, which lasts until 1:00 PM. After church we come home, unplug the phones, and disconnect. We sit down to lunch, light candles, and say a prayer together. Over lunch we may talk about what happened that day in church or ask our daughters what they learned in Sunday school. After lunch, we go into the family room and read, then either nap or play. Sometimes we take the dog on a long walk. Or we may play a board game or jump on the trampoline.

At around 5:00 PM we go back to church for the evening service, then come home and relax before bed. We try to run all of our errands (including going to the grocery store and the gas station) *before* Sunday so that we aren't tempted to play catch-up on our Sabbath day. We don't turn on the television or the stereo or log on to the computer to check e-mails. We try to spend some time in reflection, even though that is hard to do with young children!

In a sense, we are taking small steps toward observing a full day of Sabbath rest. We are not there by a long shot, so please don't miss the point: start where you are. To decide to unplug for three hours may be a great place to start. How far you choose to go is up to you, but consider how compelling some of the Sabbath "rules" are for you: you are not allowed to worry on the Sabbath, you are not allowed to plan on the Sabbath, you are not allowed to work. You can just *be* for a change.

When we began this Sabbath practice, I had no idea of the impact it would make on our family. Honestly, I had become so used to a seven-day-a-week schedule that a Sabbath day seemed impossible. Today, I could not live without it. Practicing the Sabbath has become a major part of my relationship with God. It gives my mind, body, and spirit a day of rest, and that rest overflows into the next week, and the next. And it's all about grace— in practicing a Sabbath I've realized how much I rely on God's grace for absolutely everything, not just salvation.

In addition to this wonderful practice of a full day of rest, you should also consider incorporating a Sabbath hour into one or two days of your week or cultivate Sabbath moments of rest throughout the other days of the week. Author Matthew Kelly (www.MatthewKelly.org) offered this collection of Sabbath moments that could, taken together, easily comprise a full day. Taken alone, they offer some wonderful opportunities for brief pockets of rest.

Read one of those books you have been meaning to read for years.

Spend time with your family.

Take an afternoon nap.

Paint a picture.

Play catch with your son.

Spend time with your friends.

Start a journal.

Just sit and listen to music. If you can play, play.

Go fishing.

Plant a garden.

Spend time with children.

Hike.

Laugh a little.

Go to a play.

Visit a museum or an art gallery.

Listen.

Swim.

Befriend silence.

Walk in the park.

Watch a sunset.

Listen to the rain.

Call your mother.

Are you getting the idea? Can you imagine the wonderful overflow of peace and rest that could come to you if you would begin to incorporate this idea of Sabbath living, even one moment at a time? Think of the renewal, refreshment, nourishment, healing, blessing, celebration, and delight in store if you started, even in a small way, today! You can enjoy the spirit of the Sabbath apart from an entire day of deliberate rest.

We want you to experience this rest because we are convinced it is foundational to all the other ways God wants to bring peace and sanity to your life. And we're also convinced there will never be a better time than now to begin.

WHAT IF . . .

. . . you dared to take God at His word and take a full day off for physical and spiritual rest?

. . . you actually unplugged all your technological toys for a day—could you imagine the impact?

. . . you took a full day off from running errands and doing chores to simply spend time with friends, family, and God?

FIVE

THE PRACTICE OF SOLITUDE AND SILENCE

*The sole cause of man's unhappiness is that he doesn't know
how to stay quietly alone in his room.*
—BLAISE PASCAL

Margo requested an appointment with me, complaining of a general, nagging sense of uneasiness—what I as a counselor would term "underlying, low-grade anxiety." She was unable to pinpoint a particular cause for her concern, but as she shared more of her history with me, one thing became evident: she simply could not disengage from the constant, external stimuli of her world.

From the moment she got up in the morning until she fell asleep at night, Margo was plugged in. Her days began with the sound of a radio blasting and ended as she dozed off to the voices of Leno and Letterman. In the hours between sleeping and waking, she was on the phone nonstop conducting business or was talking between sales calls with her many coworkers. During her commute she played a shuffled assortment of her favorite CDs constantly. She chattered with colleagues through lunch and met up with friends soon after work.

As we talked further about her routine, a light came on for Margo. "I think I'm afraid to be alone with myself," she said. "For me, there's something downright scary about solitude and silence."

Most of us are more like Margo than we care to admit. Even while our patterns of constant noise and stimulation are producing in us their own brand of stress, we seem to prefer *that* unease to the unease we imagine we would feel if we stopped! Few of us today would deliberately choose solitude or silence. The idea just seems, as Margo put it, a little too "scary" or weird.

But we strongly disagree. In fact, we're willing to argue that those set-apart spaces of solitude and silence are precisely *where* all the good stuff happens—or at least where we are prepared to receive and appreciate the good, the true, and the beautiful things of life. Solitude and silence are not only instructive; they can actually be *transforming* if we will only try them.

FORCED OR CHOSEN?

Sometimes we are forced into solitude by unforeseen circumstances, but whether we choose solitude or it is chosen for us, it has great power to transform us. Remember the movie *Castaway*? In it, Tom Hanks played a busy FedEx executive named Chuck, who survives a plane crash on Christmas Eve. After plummeting into the ocean during a terrifying storm, Chuck is washed up on an island—utterly and completely alone. For the next four years, this hard-charging, make-it-happen guy is marooned with no company at all, except a volleyball he names Wilson. Finally, he constructs a raft and is rescued, but when he returns to his old life, he is clearly a different man with different priorities. Something happened to Chuck in solitude that would not have happened otherwise, even though he did not choose his lonely circumstances.

Solitude and silence also transform those who willingly choose it. Perhaps none so powerfully demonstrate this as the saints from centuries ago known as the Desert Fathers. These fourth- and fifth-century mystics became disillusioned with modern life and followed God's call into the desert. One of them, a young man named Anthony, left the comforts of Egyptian civilization and withdrew into the desert wilderness for twenty years. *Twenty years!* Anthony emerged from his self-appointed solitude with a depth, an authenticity, and a spirituality that far surpassed any maturity the peers of his youth had acquired through the years. People came from near and far to hear Anthony speak with clarity, grace, and humility of what he learned in solitude. Later in life he returned to the desert, and it must have suited him well: he died there at the ripe old age of 106!

WHY PRACTICE SOLITUDE?

One fictional man was forced into solitude. One historical man chose it. Both were transformed by it. And if we dig deeper into their individual stories, we see another common denominator between the two of them: the need for relationship. Chuck made friends with a volleyball and gave it a name because he needed to communicate, even in his solitude. Anthony used his desert time to communicate with his God. Both instances illustrate the fact that we are relational beings made to interact, and even in solitude, we will do so. So if we are relational beings, why would solitude ever be necessary? There are many reasons.

We Are Prone to Drift

The first reason we need solitude is that it can keep us on course with God. Our castaway friend Chuck was never really alone on his island. Anthony was never really alone in the desert. Even in their remote outposts, each had access to the one relationship that matters most: a relationship with God. We have the same access, but how often do we let life and busyness and people crowd in on us so that this relationship drifts from the center of our lives? Robert Robinson, who wrote the great hymn "Come, Thou Fount of Every Blessing," expressed it like this: "Prone to wander, Lord, I feel it / Prone to leave the God I love." Our natural tendency is to wander from the love of God, but solitude allows us to turn down the volume of our culture and more clearly hear His still, small voice.

Modern writer Gary Thomas, in *Sacred Pathways,* spoke very candidly about this practice and sees solitude as the anchor of his God-directed life:

> Over the years, solitude has become one of my best friends. There is a quiet and depth to solitude that nourishes me while other spiritual activities—preaching, for instance—deplete me. Even in a crowd or party, sometimes I'll try to "sneak in" a few moments of solitude. Some might argue that in doing this I'm taking myself too seriously, and they may be right. All I know is that it's in those solitary moments that colors regain their brightness, truth regains its clarity, and reality loses its fog. Without some time alone, I feel like I've lost my anchor.

Solitude draws us back to the things of God when we have wandered from them. It allows us to ponder the truths God is revealing, puts them in perspective, and makes room for us to enjoy God's creation and relish His goodness to us.

It also insulates us, to some degree, from the demands and lures of everyday life. Listen to how Saint Paul instructed his friends to resist the overwhelming demands of this world:

> So here's what I want you to do, God helping you: Take your everyday, ordinary life—your sleeping, eating, going-to-work, and walking-around life—and place it before God as an offering. Embracing what God does for you is the best thing you can do for him. Don't become so well-adjusted to your culture that you fit in without even thinking. Instead, fix your attention on God. You'll be changed from the inside out. Readily recognize what he wants from you, and quickly respond to it. Unlike the culture around you, always dragging you down to its level of immaturity, God brings the best out of you, develops well-formed maturity in you. (Romans 12:1–2 THE MESSAGE)

Do you see his point? If we don't actively "fix [our] attention" on God to the exclusion of other things, we'll eventually be swept away in the cultural current to the detriment of our values, our voices, and our impact. In other words, instead of influencing our culture for the cause of Christ, our culture will influence us for its own purposes.

Now don't get us wrong: we're not anticulture. We need to celebrate and embrace some aspects and reform other aspects of the world in which we live. It is in solitude, however—in purposeful times spent in the presence of God—where we learn to discern what to embrace and what to reform. In solitude we realize our call to be transformed people, so that through Christ we may transform the world.

WE ARE DESIGNED FOR COMMUNITY

Also, we need the practice of solitude because *God designed us for community.* We realize this may seem like a contradictory statement, so let us explain. If we do not spend time alone with God, finding *in Him* our security and identity, we are almost certain to muck up our relationships with others by focusing too much on our own neediness.

Spiritual writer Henri Nouwen explained it like this:

> Without the solitude of heart our relationships with each other, with others, easily become needy, greedy, sticky and clinging, dependent, sentimental, exploitative, and parasitic because without the solitude of heart we cannot experience others as different from ourselves but only as people who can be used for the fulfillment of our own often hidden needs.

Those who cannot be alone and find themselves constantly seeking the company of others can actually end up sucking the life out of those closest to them! God deals with us individually before He deals with us in community. When we draw our strength from time spent alone with Him, we are satisfied in our inner selves and are in a much better position to love others selflessly.

Dietrich Bonhoeffer, a young German theologian executed by the Nazis shortly before the end of World War II, said as much:

Let him who cannot be alone beware of community. He will do harm to himself and to the community. Alone you stood before God when he called you, alone you had to answer that call, alone you had to struggle and pray and alone you will die and give an account to God. You cannot escape from yourself, for God has singled you out.

If you desire to be fully present in all your relationships (and most people will say they do!) you need times of solitude. I want to be all there for my wife. I want to be there for my kids. I want to be there for the friends God has blessed me with, as well as for the people that I am trying to reach out to. God places certain people in our lives—those with whom we live, work, attend school, church—for a purpose, and the only way we can realize and fulfill that purpose is by spending time alone with Christ. We need His love, His wisdom, His perspective, and His grace to best relate to others.

We Need Refining

We need the practice of solitude because we are prone to drift and because we are made for community. But we also need solitude because *we need refining*. We're flawed creatures who struggle against selfish desires and prideful actions. Most of the time, it takes solitude to break our wills and help us to die to our compulsions. Paul talked about this kind of dying in a letter to his friends in the church at Colossae.

Therefore put to death your members which are on the earth: fornication, uncleanness, passion, evil desire, and covetousness, which is idolatry. Because of these things the wrath of God is coming upon the sons of disobedience, in which you yourselves once walked when you lived in them. But now you yourselves are to put off all these: anger, wrath, malice, blasphemy, filthy language out of your mouth. Do not lie to one another, since you have put off the old man with his deeds, and have put on the new man who is renewed in knowledge according to the image of Him who created him. (Colossians 3:5–10 NKJV)

In solitude, we see where we've messed up. With no distractions, we are able to confess our shortcomings and realize that we cannot please God on our own. In solitude, we can die to our old selves and ask Him, by His Spirit, to help us live holy lives.

Now, no one's old sinful self dies without a fight, and we will not be completely transformed until we see God face-to-face. But the fact that holy living will always be a struggle doesn't mean we have a license to quit striving. We need to be participants in God's refining process, and that process often begins in solitude. Henri Nouwen called solitude "the place of the great struggle and the great encounter, the struggle against the compulsion of the false self and the encounter with the loving God who offers himself as the substance of the new self."

You and I can't abide solitude without the love of Christ, because without Him, we would be hopeless to change the things we see in ourselves that need changing. But with Him, solitude is a precious, wonderful thing. In it, we see that He loves us no matter what and is never driven away by the sight of our authentic selves. And through this love, new life is available to us: not just the new life that we receive upon salvation, but a new and refined life, to be lived here on earth.

A Loving Father Beckons

Finally, we need solitude because *a loving Father beckons*. Solitude isn't a soundless vacuum. It's the most intimate of all relationships: a relationship with our Father.

Last week I went to a play-off baseball game. I had prime diamond box seats right behind home plate. Great seats, but I didn't get any of the usual free food, and no celebrities sat next to me. It was actually a play-off game for coach-pitched first graders.

There was a very exciting moment in the game, a critical turning point. A confident three-foot-five batter stepped up to the plate with a runner named Thomas on first. I walked over to the third baseline, hoping for an exciting play. As Thomas was anxiously waiting on first base, his teammate got a hit. *Crack.* The kid hit the ball into the outfield and ran for first base. Thomas took off from first. He was cruising around second base, approaching third. All the coaches and spectators in the stands were yelling, "Stop, Thomas. Stop! Don't go! Stop, Thomas! Don't go!" And as he was heading for third, he heard one lone voice in the stands saying, "Goooo, Thomas! Run, Thomas, run!" So without looking back, Thomas passed up third and made his way all the way to home plate, scoring a very thrilling run for the team.

Now why in the world did that little first-grader do that with the multitudes crying out, "No! Stop, Thomas! Stop, stop, stop!" and one dissenting voice saying, "Go!"? Why? Simple. He heard the voice of his father above all others.

Thomas had learned even in the heat of the game, when the

pressure was on, to hear and discern the voice of his father over all the other voices shouting at him.

If we are going to make it in the real world, we have to learn to hear our Father's voice over all the other voices shouting and screaming at us in the culture.

Because Jesus knew this, He often practiced solitude. Before He began His public ministry, He spent forty days of prayer and fasting in a desolate place. Before He chose His twelve disciples, He spent an entire night alone in prayer. Before He went to the cross, He prayed alone in the garden. Frequently, He rose early in the morning to spend time with His Father, even leaving the company of those He loved best to follow the call of God.

Pastor and author Calvin Miller wrote, "Where we volunteer for silence, and put our personal agendas to sleep, God comes to us, and His coming instructs our lives. Indeed, His coming becomes our life."

Last year, I had the opportunity to take a weeklong spiritual retreat (a mini-sabbatical of sorts) in order to spend time with God in nature. For this entire week I was completely unplugged: no phone, no television, no Internet, no e-mail, no fax machines, no radio, and virtually no people. Each day I filled with meditation and prayer, reading and journaling, interspersed with exercise, nature hikes, and eating, of course. One day I even devoted to a vow of silence. The best way I can describe this time is that it provided for me a much-needed emotional cleansing and spiritual renewal. It was as though I hit the "reset button." The impact of this short time has been far reaching and life changing. It helped me to reconnect with the rhythms of life, slow the pace, reestablish my true priorities, renew my thinking, and let go of old baggage. Most importantly, it set me on a deeper spiritual path with God.

Please don't miss the point. We know it's not always feasible to take weeklong spiritual retreats to faraway places. If you can pull it off, great—go for it. But if you cannot, then the spirit of this still applies. Take a day or even a weekend. One friend we know plans regular times of solitude in a retreat house several hours from her home. The house is rustic and completely void of high-tech gadgets. In fact, it's called the "quiet house." But this friend insists that although her destination is a solitary retreat, she is never alone. In fact, she relates that in driving to this place of solitude she feels a sense of expectation that she is going to meet a dearly loved Other in whose presence she delights. She's being beckoned by a loving God.

So How Does Solitude Work?

We hope we've whetted your appetite for solitude, at least a little. We understand that some personality types will find solitude easier to embrace than others. Almost every one of us leans toward being either an introvert or an extrovert. Obviously, extroverts, who find their strength and renewal by engaging with their outer world—by being around people and maintaining social connections—will find the practice of solitude much more challenging. Introverts—those who have a natural tendency toward self-examination and are renewed and energized by exploring their inner world—will more readily gravitate toward solitude and silence. Even so, every personality can benefit from the practice of solitude, and no type is naturally exempt from it. The introvert may be comfortable with longer periods of solitude, but the extrovert can and should experiment with solitude, even if those times are initially brief. Remember, just because a thing is difficult does not mean it is not worth doing!

So how does solitude work? First, we believe it's important to understand that it's okay to be a little afraid of solitude or apprehensive about trying it. Many, many people have a fear of the unknown and the unfamiliar, and if solitude is an unknown for you, you're going to feel hesitant about it. Perhaps you are so addicted to the incessant noise and constant motion of this world that you anticipate a little agitation as you venture into stillness and quiet. Give yourself permission to feel uncomfortable as you push through to experience the benefits that await you. God will be with you in your solitude, and He is more than able to handle whatever happens there.

But in all likelihood, what you encounter will not be negative, but positive. Solitude provides time for reflection, dreaming, listening, and loving: all of the good things that can happen to you can happen to you alone!

Also, you might fear the emptiness of solitude. In other words, you don't fear encountering something; you fear encountering nothing. You may wonder, *What if I don't experience anything at all? What would that say about me? Could I handle it?* The truth is, all of us experience some degree of emptiness in solitude at least some of the time. It's normal, even necessary to do so. Author Wayne Muller wrote:

> All life has emptiness at its core; it is the quiet hollow reed through which the wind of God blows and makes the music that is our life. Without this emptiness we are clogged and unable to give birth to music, love, or kindness. All creation springs from emptiness: in the beginning God created the heavens and the earth. The earth was without form and void.

Singer/songwriter David Wilcox called this emptiness "the lonely," and he said it has a special purpose:

When I feel hollow, that's just proof that there's more for me to follow—that's what the lonely is for.

As strange and counterintuitive as it seems, emptiness is the primary prerequisite for being filled!

Now, if you are ready to experiment with solitude, here are some simple steps to take.

First, intentionally pursue solitude by making time for it. That means learning to walk in the Spirit in a culture that demands that you run. Every now and then, resist those running demands. Slow down instead. Take time away. Maybe you could find some quiet time in the morning before everyone else in your house begins to stir. Or perhaps you could steal away for a little while late at night, or in the middle of the day. The actual time doesn't matter, but consistently pursuing it does. Practiced often enough, solitude will become a healthy habit, one you will not want to forgo.

> *Intentionally pursue solitude by making time for it. That means learning to walk in the Spirit in a culture that demands that you run. Every now and then, resist those running demands. Slow down instead. Take time away.*

Then you must intentionally make a place for solitude. The place you retreat to doesn't have to be miles or hours from home. It just needs to be a set-apart space where you can spend extended time with Christ without distractions. Jesus said, "When you pray, you should go into your room and close the door and pray to your Father who cannot be seen. Your Father can see what is done in secret, and He will reward you" (Matthew 6:6 NCV). In other words, make a place where family, friends, and the demands of life will not intrude.

Of course, this doesn't have to be a room in your house. It can (and ideally should) be a quiet place outside on your porch, under a tree, in a park, at the lake, wherever. It's imperative to have such a place if you mean to reap the true benefits of solitude.

Finally, you must deliberately enter into silence. Solitude and silence are partners. Mother Teresa explained the necessity of silence like this:

> God is the friend of silence. His language is silence. And he requires us to be silent to discover him. We need, therefore, silence to be alone with God, to speak to him, to listen to him and to ponder his words deep in our hearts. We need to be alone with God in silence to be renewed and to be transformed. For silence can give us a new outlook on life. In it we are filled with the grace of God, which makes us do all things with joy.

If you are going to enjoy time alone in reflection, meditation, and prayer, you must learn to be still and silent before God. Make the time. Find a place. Then enter into silence. Strive for quality over quantity. When you are consistently experiencing quality times of solitude, your desire for their quantity will naturally increase.

Enjoy the Benefits of Solitude

Early in life we're taught not to ask, "What's in it for me?" We're instructed instead to think of others and not be selfish. These are good lessons, but they don't necessarily apply to the practice of solitude. In fact, we hope you *do* ask what benefits solitude might have for you. We think you should know that there are many, and we want to share just a few of them with you:

- Solitude is *nurturing*. It is like a refuge in a storm. Solitude feels like a sanctuary of safety, security, and stability in an out-of-control world.
- Solitude is *centering*. It's a place for getting grounded, and it provides the objectivity we need to contend with the competing voices of this disorienting world. Solitude provides the opportunity to reconnect with the things that matter most and filter out those things that don't.
- Solitude is *reflecting*. It is often the place where we gain important and valuable insights about ourselves and our lives, and the changes we need to make.
- Solitude is *nourishing*. It provides fertile soil in which our relationship to God can grow. In solitude, we drink from the Father's well for our fulfillment and peace. His presence feeds us when we need it most.
- Solitude is *listening*. In a world where thousands of voices clamor for your attention, solitude enables you to hear the one that matters most. His voice is the one that offers solace and soothing and comfort, and only He can speak to us true words of life.

We encourage you to begin today to practice solitude—and to expect great things from it. Look at it this way: no one is transformed sitting in front of a plasma screen. Can someone really experience all the benefits of solitude while watching a DVD or listening to a favorite CD for the hundredth time? Yes, it is true that some film and music, like many other things, can bring us to transcendent moments, but they are *not* substitutes for solitude. No one gets the peace that passes understanding from voice mail, e-mail, or instant messaging. It is only by touching the transcendent that we are truly transformed, and solitude invites God's transcendent presence.

Are you wondering what to do in your moments of solitude and silence? We thought you might be, so we encourage you to read on. Solitude and silence set the stage for prayer and meditation, and we'll show you how to experience those important practices in the next chapter.

What If . . .

. . . you had the courage to spend some time alone in silence and solitude?

. . . you deliberately turned down the volume of this culture to tune in to the things of God?

. . . you took off for a weekend or, better yet, an entire week to put yourself in a position to truly hear from God?

SIX

THE PRACTICE OF PRESENCE

A half hour of prayer and meditation is essential except when you
are very busy—then a full hour is needed.
—FRANCIS DE SALES

Recently, I was in one of the seven Starbucks within a one-mile radius of my office, having coffee with a friend. Actually, on this particular day, I was having a pseudo-coffee drink, a Frappuccino, which costs as much as a decent lunch (I am anxious for Starbucks to come up with a Dollar Menu like McDonald's). My friend stepped away for a minute, so I was visiting with a guy who was there having coffee as well. The topic of our conversation turned to his very noticeable hairstyle: dreadlocks, á la Bob Marley. He told me that his former girlfriend, a Rastafarian, had explained to him that the dreadlocks acted as antennas to aid in receiving communication from God.

My response was to nod understandingly, pick up my drink,

take a long sip, look back at him, and say, "That's interesting, because God speaks to me through my Frappuccino. Whenever I drink Frap with a straw, I get that caffeine and sugar feeling, and that's how God speaks to me."

And the beauty of the story is that *he* laughed at *me*. As if the antenna dreadlocks method was less arbitrary and more plausible than my Frappuccino method!

People try to connect with God in many ways, but the point is that we know we need God's presence in our lives—the kind of presence that supersedes a mere knowledge of His omnipresence. But many of us mistakenly believe that *this* kind of presence, or intimacy, and the enjoyment of His company are available only to supersized saints: the disciples, or martyrs, or people like Mother Teresa, the pope, or Billy Graham. If you have that impression, we have great news for you. *You* (that's right, you!) can have an audience with the Almighty. *You* have a way in to the very throne room of heaven. You may be an ordinary man or woman, but you have extraordinary power close by, and it becomes available to you in seeking out the presence of God through the practices of prayer and meditation.

It is in solitude that our hearts are primed for the thing that we need most: the very presence of God Himself. Writer and teacher Richard Foster said it is through the contemplative practices of prayer and meditation that we "create the emotional and spiritual space which allows Christ to construct an inner sanctuary of the heart." Isn't that a comforting image, that somewhere deep inside us we could build and furnish a sanctuary for God's presence and meet with Him there? It's not only comforting; it's true.

Remember the movie *Spiderman*? You probably saw it, since it grossed more than $230 million in the box office during the first two weeks of its release. *Spiderman* had plenty of eye-popping special effects, a heroic story line, and even a romantic subplot. But some have suggested that the real genius behind the Spidey franchise was the casting of its star, Tobey Maguire. Why genius? Because Tobey Maguire doesn't look a *thing* like a superhero! He's short. He's not especially buff. And he's average looking enough to be your next-door neighbor. People like you and I could easily identify with this ordinary guy with extraordinary powers. We rooted for him because we feel mostly run-of-the-mill too, but long to have special powers and to use them for good.

In Spiderman's story, those special powers came from a random insect bite. In the spiritual realm, they come through prayer. Prayer is that process of communicating or connecting with God. It takes place when ordinary people like us begin to lean upon an extraordinary God. Our dependency plus His power equals something life changing and supernatural. In short, prayer is an essential key to tapping the infinite power and resources of God—not the least of which are His peace, His joy, and His patience (and the list goes on and on).

You've hung with us through the explorations of Sabbath and solitude. (And we're glad you did.) But perhaps now you're thinking, *Oh, boy—this is where it gets too complicated for me. I've never been any good at prayer. I try and I just feel guilty for not ever getting it right.* If that describes you, then take heart. You are close—so very close—to experiencing a life of peace, simplicity, and power.

In this chapter we will sometimes use the terms *prayer* and *meditation* interchangeably. Don't let that scare you. They are simply two sides to the coin of contemplation: focusing our hearts, minds, and bodies Godward so we may experience the awesome, life-changing presence of God.

Perhaps you are far more comfortable with the idea of praying than you are with meditating. Allow us to explain what meditation means. Meditation is not exclusively a New Age practice; in fact, it's much older than that. By *meditation* we mean specific and intentional focus on the things of God (His truth, His Word, His character, His attributes) for the purpose of intimately connecting with Him. In fact, the word *meditation* comes from the Latin root "to ponder," and so to meditate on God is to ponder what concerns Him. This practice has always been a central part of Christian spirituality, and Scripture is full of references to it. (Still not sure? Check out Psalm 63:6–7; Genesis 24:63; Psalm 119:97–101; and Philippians 4:8 from the New King James Version.)

That said, we strongly believe in the practices of prayer and meditation. Prayer is absolutely essential for the Christ-follower. Without it, we are subject to the whims of emotion, and we are at the mercy of our circumstances. Prayer is so central that without it, life makes no sense. I love what Russian theologian Vasili Rozanov once said: "There is no life without prayer. Without prayer there is only madness and horror. The soul of Orthodoxy consists in the gift of prayer." In a certain sense, it is through prayer that we maintain our sanity in this crazy, chaotic world of ours. We believe that we can have no inner peace and no outward simplicity without prayer, and that our lives are stripped of the power we desperately need if we consistently fail to connect with God through prayer.

This nonnegotiable practice simply *must* become a part of your life, even if you have to start small. We believe that just a taste of the riches of prayer and meditation will leave you wanting more. And in this case, it's perfectly okay to work up an insatiable appetite!

Charles Spurgeon said it like this:

He who lives without prayer, he who lives with little prayer, he who seldom reads the Word, and he who seldom looks up to heaven for a fresh influence from on high—he will be the man whose heart will become dry and barren. However, he who falls in secret on his God, who spends much time in holy retirement, who delights to meditate on the words of the Most High, and whose soul is given up to Christ— such a man must have an overflowing heart. As his heart is, such will be his life.

Six Ways Prayer Helps Us "Practice the Presence"

First and foremost, the main reason we pray is to get into the presence of God where we have access to His power, His peace, His love, His friendship, and more. Choosing to pray is one of the wisest and healthiest things we can do to experience God's presence— and His peace. Here's why:

1. Prayer Supplies Protection

The apostle Paul alluded to this when he wrote to his friends at Philippi: "Be anxious for nothing, but in everything by prayer and supplication, with thanksgiving, let your requests be made known to God; and the peace of God, which surpasses all understanding, will guard your hearts and minds through Christ Jesus" (Philippians 4:6–7 NKJV). Paul encouraged them to pray because he knew that through prayer, the peace of God would come to guard their hearts and minds!

The same Greek word Paul used for "guard" also described the Roman centurion who stood watch outside the palace of the governor. Imagine a mighty soldier, dressed out in full armor, bearing a sword, a spear, and a shield. Now imagine that imposing guard as the very peace of God, keeping watch over *your* heart and *your* mind. Sounds good, doesn't it? It is—and prayer affords us that kind of protection.

> *Isn't worry just a form of communication with ourselves about our problems? So, as we channel our worry into prayer, we are changing the direction of our conversation from ourselves back toward God.*

By the way, this formula offers a cure for circumstantial anxiety. After all, isn't worry just a form of communication with ourselves about our problems? So, as we channel our worry into prayer, we are changing the direction of our conversation from ourselves back toward God.

2. PRAYER TEACHES DEPENDENCY

The heart of prayer, more than anything else, is dependency and trust. When we pray we are admitting that we cannot manage our lives by ourselves—that we cannot leverage the world or cause it to move on our behalf. When we pray we are acknowledging that God's strength is not merely something nice; it's something that is absolutely necessary. Consider, for example, the symbolism associated with the prayer posture of laying ourselves before God or falling on our knees: that's humility and dependency in their purest forms.

The prophet Isaiah wrote:

Do you not know? Have you not heard?
The Everlasting God, the LORD, the Creator of the ends of
     the earth
Does not become weary or tired.
His understanding is inscrutable.
He gives strength to the weary,
And to him who lacks might He increases power.
(Isaiah 40:28–29 NASB)

Through prayer, we learn dependency on the mighty power of God. We need Him. And we need to be reminded that we do.

3. Prayer Encourages Listening

Every conversation has two parts: speaking and listening. Generally, most of us are terrible listeners. What we call "listening" could more accurately be described as "getting ready to speak again." But prayer requires that we learn to listen, because God is and has always been a God who speaks. He has spoken through His prophets. He has spoken through His Son. He speaks through His Word, through creation, and through the still, small voice of His Holy Spirit. God is speaking 24/7. When we pray, we are encouraged to become better listeners, because God has a lot to say.

Many people pray without any real expectation of actually hearing from God, and yet God is actively speaking to those who have the spiritual ears to hear. Would you even dare to imagine the benefits of adding this important dimension to your spiritual life?

4. PRAYER OFFERS FREEDOM

There aren't too many places in life where we are free to be ourselves with no pretense, to openly express our thoughts without subterfuge or censor. Prayer is that kind of place. C. S. Lewis once advised a friend to pray as he was, not as he thought he ought to be. Likewise, we have a close friend who often says, "Don't try to be more spiritual than you are. Just be yourself." In prayer, we are free to come before God as we are and to leave with Him whatever we will. In His presence we can let go of our controlling grip and know the freedom of surrender and release.

5. PRAYER INVITES TRANSFORMATION

Prayer doesn't change God. He is immutable, unchangeable. Prayer changes us, because we are the ones who need changing! Prayer can give us, sometimes in a matter of seconds, the energy, understanding, and patience we need to cope with the challenges of life.

Suppose you are in the midst of an intense conflict with your spouse, a friend, or a loved one. Tension is high; anger, aggression, and turmoil prevail. Then the telephone rings, and it is your sick mother calling from her hospital bed. She is alone and afraid and needs your reassurance. You know from experience that you will somehow be able to change your mood and demeanor very quickly, so that you can calmly and compassionately speak with her as if no argument had just taken place. You'll dig down deep or do some fast mental maneuvering to get yourself to a place of rationality and calmness.

In the same way, our circumstances may not change instantly with prayer, but our state of mind and heart can! God's tranquility can replace our anxiety; His peace can transcend our panic. Prayer wrung out of us by our deepest needs transforms us because through it, we access what we already possess: the indwelling power and presence of God through Christ and His Holy Spirit.

6. PRAYER ESTABLISHES PERSPECTIVE

In prayer we are reminded that something and Someone exists beyond this world; there is another reality on the other side of the veil, and through the lens of prayer we come to understand our existence in the context of a greater reality. Madam Guyon, a seventeenth-century mystic who was once a wealthy French socialite (the Paris Hilton of her day), came to enjoy a relationship with God that allowed her to say, "I love God more than the most affectionate lover loves the object of his [or her] earthly attachment . . . The amusements and pleasures which are so much prized and esteemed by the world now appear to me dull and insipid, so much that I wondered how I could have ever enjoyed them."

Prayer enabled her to establish a new perspective. She could no longer view her world in the same way.

PRACTICING THE PRESENCE OF GOD

Brother Lawrence was a seventeenth-century monk who learned to "practice the presence" of God. Throughout the normal routine of his day, washing pots and pans in a monastery kitchen, he developed the ability to maintain an ongoing conversation with God. Through the practice of God's presence, even the most mundane tasks became sacred acts of worship. He lived out Paul's challenge in 1 Thessalonians 5:17 (NKJV) to "pray without ceasing," but he only occasionally closed his eyes and bowed his head! He was conscious of God's abiding presence throughout the course of his day.

Jesus' life demonstrated this continual awareness of God's presence too. His disciples no doubt noticed and envied it when they asked Him, "Lord, teach us to pray" (Luke 11:1 NKJV). Now, they knew more than a little about prayer. They'd known the Jewish traditions and practices regarding prayer since childhood, and they had surely memorized many prayers in their lifetimes. But they didn't have what Jesus had, and they wanted it. They weren't so much asking for a how-to manual on prayer as they were asking Him, "Lord, teach us to pray: to speak with the Father and know and enjoy Him the way You do." It was intimacy they were after, not a script.

Jesus answered their request by giving them an example—but He never meant for it to be their *only* prayer. He knew that they hungered to experience the relationship He had with the Father, not just to mouth the words He spoke in private. He also knew that they would have to learn to experience God's presence on their own, and that, at times, the sample prayer He offered would even be replaced by a complete lack of words (see Romans 8:26 NKJV). But all this would take time and practice.

Imagine watching two people dancing in perfect rhythm. You envy their grace, and you wonder how you could possibly learn to move like that. Despite your two left feet, you ask them to teach you. How helpful would it be for them to give you a book with steps outlined, suggest that you go home and read all about it, then come back in a week and show them what you learned? Not very. In the same way, it certainly isn't very helpful to learn to play golf by simply watching Tiger Woods or by reading up on his technique.

It's not possible to learn to dance or to play golf in any way but by doing it. In the same way, we learn best to pray by praying. For this reason, we aren't the least bit interested in giving you a step-by-step manual on prayer and meditation. There is no foolproof training protocol for becoming a man or woman who practices the presence of God. But there are principles and practices that can help us cultivate a joy-filled preoccupation with Him, and we will share just a few of them with you here.

FOCUS ON IMPACT, NOT ACTION

First, remember that prayer and meditation are *inner* disciplines: don't make the mistake of equating action with impact. Prayer may seem passive, and meditation may appear nebulous, but these are practices of enormous impact. Henri Nouwen said:

> We listen to sermons and the affirming benefits of a life of communion with God, but somewhere deep down we believe that it is action, not prayer and meditation, that will actually satisfy our needs. We may think prayer is good when there is nothing more important to do, but we have strong reservations and doubts about God's effectiveness in our world.

Not too long ago, during a difficult personal struggle, I recall desperately having searched for answers from a wise friend. I fully expected a long, philosophical explanation of my circumstances, and I was prepared for a lot of advice and wisdom. The only thing he said, however, was, "Pray, pray, pray." I went away feeling slightly disappointed but willing to try.

As it turned out, prayer was the only thing that got me through that dark time and gave me perspective and light. The results of our one-on-one time with God are not always readily visible, but they are real. Go for impact over impulsive action. Decide to patiently and faithfully invest the time it takes to know God well.

CONSIDER IT A PROCESS, NOT A PROJECT

Prayer and meditation are not finite projects—items to check off your to-do list. Together they form a process, a way of life.

> *Prayer and meditation are not finite projects— items to check off your to-do list. Together they form a process, a way of life.*

Instead of thinking of them as something you do for ten minutes each morning, think outside the box. Look for opportunities to pray or meditate throughout the day. Pray in the car or the shower, or while gardening or exercising.

Pray when you are "up" and when you are feeling down in the dumps. Pray for others when God brings them to mind, not when you've accumulated enough of a list to make praying for others seem efficient. Invite God to bring your work to life so that the ordinary can be transformed into something extraordinary. Pray for those you come into contact with each day, even strangers.

Develop an eye for the creative hand of God, so that when you walk or drive you notice and meditate on what He has made. Then thank Him for the beauty of His creation each time you encounter it.

Praying in this way is not like snacking. It doesn't spoil your appetite for longer, more extended times with God. It makes you hungrier for them. And regardless of the reasons and the content of our prayers, a funny thing happens when we pray: we usually get the added blessing of His peace.

JUST BREATHE

Breathing is the most natural, instinctive thing we do, but intentional focus on breathing can have an enormous impact on our daily lives and our devotional lives. We know this may sound strange, but proper breathing is foundational for a life of peace. The truth is, our breathing patterns influence our physical symptoms. That's why breathing is a core component of most exercise, relaxation, and stress-management programs. When we are hurried, stressed, or agitated, our breathing becomes shallow and quick. By deliberately slowing our breathing and doing it more deeply, we can quickly become more calm and focused. That's why most great athletes, musicians, and speakers practice some ritual of deep breathing just before they go out to perform.

When you use breathing to calm your mind and quiet your heart, you help yourself to a place where God, not your trouble, is your primary focus. Try this breathing exercise (right now), and see how it affects you:

1. Sit in a quiet, comfortable position.
2. Take a long, slow breath in through your nose, filling your abdomen (lower lungs) and then your chest (upper lungs).
3. Hold that breath to the count of three.
4. Gently, slowly, and fully exhale through your mouth while you relax your body.

There's no magic here, nothing complicated whatsoever. But this way of relaxing can help you center and focus your heart and your thoughts Godward in just a few moments' time. Once you are fully relaxed and centered, you can say to yourself, *With each breath, I am taking in the very breath of God.* Wait for Him to fill you with His presence. Anticipate refreshment and renewal as you begin to feel His peace and comfort. Go ahead, spend a few moments and try it.

We want you to become intimately familiar with the practice of breath work with an emphasis on slow, deep, and intentional breathing. It may be difficult initially to fully appreciate the value of proper and focused breathing, but trust us on this. The more you can incorporate this practice into your daily life, the more equipped you will be to manage the stress and get to a calm place to truly experience the presence of God.

In fact, the benefits are so valuable, we are convinced that if you would genuinely pursue and learn to integrate this meditative practice into your daily routine, this alone would *radically* alter your life for the better: we guarantee it! So remember that anytime you begin to feel overwhelmed or anxious, regardless of the situation, you've got a powerful resource at your disposal: stop for a minute, invite God's presence, and just breathe!

DON'T BE SQUEAMISH ABOUT THE M-WORD

Eastern meditative practices seek to empty the mind of all rational thought. The emphasis there is on detachment for detachment's sake, not on engagement. Christian meditation, on the other hand, emphasizes detachment from the noise and distraction of this world so that we may "attach" to God by filling our minds with His truth.

Truthfully, we are all skilled in this art of deliberate focus. For example, some of us are very skilled in ruminating over negative things and worrying. Others of us are able to focus very intently on sports or the stock market. It is the object of our meditation that makes the most difference. We challenge you to extend your focus toward the things of God, moving beyond intellectual knowledge to experiential understanding.

I (Sam) know certain facts about my wife: she has big, brown eyes, she likes Italian cream cake, she was born in Austin, Texas, and so on. But the privilege of marriage allows me to focus more deeply and intentionally on her so that, in addition to the facts I know about her, I am able to experience and appreciate her in a more complete way: emotionally, physically, and spiritually. That kind of knowing is the intent of meditation, and it is nothing to be afraid of when the object of our devotion is God Himself!

Appreciating the Value of Prayer and Meditation

Some twenty years ago while attending college, I was introduced to a book called *The Celebration of Discipline* by Richard Foster. I completely devoured it. In fact, I can't think of a single resource that has had a greater impact on my spiritual life than this one. It was the primary catalyst in launching me toward a deeper walk with God, and it literally changed my life from the inside out.

In a sense, Foster normalized the use of the classical spiritual disciplines of silence, simplicity, prayer, fasting, and worship by making them seem accessible and new, not ethereal and ancient. But, more importantly, he suggested that these disciplines are not some dull drudgery but a joy; not a duty but a privilege.

We want you to experience the delight and deep satisfaction that come from spending time in the presence of God. We're advocating prayer and meditation *not* because they'll make you some kind of super-Christian, but because they'll satisfy your hunger and thirst. We acknowledge that we live in a culture that is not hip to the contemplative life.

There is virtually nothing about our times that encourages or supports intentional focus on the heart of God. But listen, friends: this is where all the good stuff is! So be patient with yourself while you experiment. Don't get caught up in guilt when you neglect spending time in God's presence. Consistently and willingly return as often as you can, by whatever means you can.

The short prayers and meditation exercises at the end of this chapter may help you to enter into His presence—and if they do, great. But they are not the end or aim of prayer and meditation. God is. Seek Him at all costs. He is the treasure beyond all treasures.

SHORT PRAYERS

A PRAYER OF SURRENDER

Oh Lord, all things that are in heaven and earth are Thine. I desire to offer myself to Thee willingly and freely to be Thine forever. In the simplicity of my heart, I offer myself to Thee this day. (Thomas à Kempis, *The Imitation of Christ*)

THE LORD'S PRAYER

Our Father in heaven,
Reveal who you are.
Set the world right;

Do what's best—
> as above, so below.

Keep us alive with three square meals.

Keep us forgiven with you and forgiving others.

Keep us safe from ourselves and the Devil.

You're in charge!

You can do anything You want!

You're ablaze in beauty!

Yes. Yes. Yes.

(Matthew 6:9–13 THE MESSAGE)

THE SERENITY PRAYER

God, grant me the serenity to accept the things I cannot change, the courage to change the things I can, and the wisdom to know the difference.

THE JESUS PRAYER

Lord Jesus Christ, Son of God, have mercy on me a sinner.

A PRAYER OF REPENTANCE

Generous in love—God give grace!

Huge in mercy—wipe out my bad record.

Scrub away my guilt;
> soak out my sins in your laundry.

I know how bad I've been;
> my sins are staring me down.

You're the One I've violated, and you've seen
> it all, seen the full extent of my evil.

You have all the facts before you;
    whatever you decide about me is fair.
I've been out of step with you for a long time,
    in the wrong since before I was born.
What you're after is truth from the inside out.
    Enter me, then; conceive a new, true life.
(Psalm 51:1–7 THE MESSAGE)

A PRAYER FOR MATURE BELIEVERS ONLY

Father, I abandon myself into your hands. Do with me whatever you will. Whatever you may do, I thank you. I am ready for all, I accept all. Let only your will be done in me, and in all your creatures. Into your hands I commend my spirit. I offer it to you with all the love that is in my heart. For I love you, Lord, and so want to give myself, to surrender myself into your hands without reserve and with boundless confidence, for you are my Father. Amen.
(Charles de Foucauld)

PRAYER AND MEDITATION PRACTICES

PRAYER OF RELEASE

In this exercise, spend a period of time releasing all your concerns into the sovereign hands of God. For example, you might start by listing your current fears and worries by name; visualize handing each one over to God. Next, move to those things you are trying to control and do the same. Then lift up your relationships, again, placing each person by name into the hands of God. Finally move into any personal habits or items you are holding on to, for example, "God, I release to you my pride [or reputation, goals, dreams, agendas]."

PRAYER WALKING

This wonderful activity involves both exercise and intense focus. The idea is to consider an image or theme (the attributes of God, or forgiveness) and spend an entire thirty-minute walk praying about it. If at any point your mind wanders, gently redirect to your original theme. You can also do this with a passage of Scripture, considering a specific phrase or truth. Not only do you get the benefits of exercise, but your soul is strengthened too!

PALMS UP/PALMS DOWN

This exercise requires you to sit comfortably, resting your hands in your lap. With your palms down, symbolic of release, let go of concerns and circumstances beyond your control. With your palms up, symbolic of receiving, receive from God His patience, love, joy, peace, kindness, self-control, and other benefits.

SPIRITUAL JOURNALING

This exercise externalizes your thoughts by committing them to paper. For some who are used to being very open, this may be basic, but for others it could revolutionize their lives! When we get things out, we tend to feel relieved. When we have fears and inner turmoil, when we are stressed or struggling with a big decision, there is tremendous value in getting our emotions and thoughts out and onto the page, where we can release them and pray over them instead of fighting against them.

What If . . .

. . . you dared to believe that maybe, just maybe, prayer actually works?

. . . you began to consciously practice the presence of God throughout your entire day?

. . . you allowed yourself to experience the full blessings of God's peace and His perspective through prayer and meditation?

THREE MOVEMENTS FOR LIFESTYLE CHANGE

We've said before that this is not your average self-help book. And you'll have to admit, up to this point, we haven't asked you to *do* much. The changes we've suggested for finding peace and simplicity have largely been internal ones: alterations in attitudes more than in actions. We've asked you to reject the idea of self-sufficiency and to entertain what, for some, may be new ideas of Sabbath rest, solitude, and the practice of God's presence.

By now, we hope you're beginning to understand that the concept of total control is a total illusion, and that our only hope for lasting peace is to release our relentless need for control into the capable hands of God. We also hope that you're starting to see how incorporating these very old "new" ideas into your everyday life can make room for God to accomplish His peace-giving work in you.

Cultivating a life of peace and simplicity in our fast-paced world is, above all, a spiritual endeavor. At its very heart, it requires our deliberate and intentional responsiveness to God's life-giving initiative—but we may also reinforce it with some moves on our part. In this section, we're giving those of you who have been itching to do something, something to do. (Is anyone saying, "Finally!"?)

These next three chapters will challenge you to minimize your stress, cut back on your overwhelming flood of activities, and enhance your capacity to receive and enjoy the good things of God. Don't worry: we're not about to load you up on to-do's, techniques, or strategies. Instead, we're going to offer some practical and simple *power moves* that can outwardly express the inward changes you've already begun to make. They won't work on their own; they need heart change to be effective. But applying them with a new mind and heart can go a long way toward helping you realize the life you were meant to live.

We're calling these strategic actions "power moves" not because they require superhuman power to accomplish, but because we believe doing them will empower you. Each has the potential to radically alter your lifestyle in a positive way.

The first power move is to *move your priorities*. We want to inspire you to be more assertive and courageous in saying no and setting boundaries. The pressure to have it all and do it all will never disappear. Never. Therefore, what must change is the way we respond to that pressure. The power move of prioritizing involves understanding and intentionally operating out of a sound worldview. It's about authentic living with an eternal focus and the freedom that can bring.

The second power move is a *move away from technology*. I'm sure this sounds like heresy to some of you, but let me give you an example of how positive it can be. I (Sam) have an afternoon ritual that involves my two-year-old son. Each day when I come in from work, I take Andrew out into our backyard and push him on the swing. Sometimes I take not only Andrew, but the cordless phone, and make personal calls during our swing time. (It's very difficult to resist the ever-present temptation to multitask.) While this may seem efficient, it keeps me from being fully present with my sweet little boy who, even at two years of age, knows when he's being shortchanged.

One afternoon some months ago, I instinctively grabbed the phone and headed with Andrew out the door. When he saw it, he turned to me, put his hands on his hips, and blurted, "No tefone! No tefone!" My wife, who saw the whole thing, smiled and said, "Ooohh—you got busted!" Needless to say, I've stopped using the cordless, and now my little guy gets my full and undivided attention when he swings. My priorities were skewed in this instance, and my use of technology was a little misguided. It's not anymore. We want you to see how moving away from technology in some instances can improve your life.

The third power move is a *move into community.* Achieving a life of peace and simplicity is not a solo venture. Sure, we want you to experience these things, but you won't experience them in a vacuum, and you're not meant to. In fact, this is part of what solitude is for: to prepare us to bring something better to others in community. There aren't too many monks in our culture these days, and we suspect we're not writing to them. We're writing to, and for, ordinary people like us, who must live and love and work and function in a culture that is not conducive to peace. And we do that in community. We want you to discover how community reflects the relational nature of God, as well as how we can be helped and help others to a life of peace and simplicity by cultivating community ourselves.

So, are you ready? Let's get moving . . .

SEVEN

MOVE YOUR PRIORITIES

Besides the noble art of getting things done, there is the
noble art of leaving things undone. Some wisdom of life consists
in the elimination of nonessentials.
—LIN YUTANG

An avid sports fan attending his first Super Bowl was seated high in the cheap seats when he noticed an empty seat down on the front row, fifty-yard line. He made his way to the spot and hopefully asked the gentleman next to the empty seat if it belonged to anyone.

"No," the man said, "no one is sitting here. I bought this ticket for my wife, but she passed away. Would you like to join me?"

"Of course I would," the sports fan replied, "but didn't you have any other friends you wanted to invite?"

"Sure," the elderly man replied. "I have lots of friends and I called them all—but they couldn't come because they're attending my wife's funeral!"

Underlying all humor is a grain of truth. We laugh at this guy because we can identify on some level with his misplaced priorities, extreme though they are. We all struggle with priorities from time to time. Throughout this book we've advocated the proactive practice of the spiritual disciplines as a way for God to transform us from the inside out, bringing us the peace and simplicity we long for. To a great degree, the practice of disciplines such as prayer and solitude and silence is an inward one, but we can just as legitimately focus on the external world and our activity in it in order to maximize outer simplicity. So now let's marry the practice of the disciplines to some practical wisdom and see what kind of impact this tandem approach can bring.

The Need for Intentional Living

Life is short, and you and I are as fragile as a mist that appears for a brief time and then evaporates (James 4:14). I know it doesn't seem like that. I know it feels as if we have all the time in the world to set priorities and live accordingly. But we don't. Existentialism (a word almost as hard to spell as it is to grasp) is a philosophical attitude based upon the reality of individual existence. It is primarily concerned with self-awareness, personal responsibility, and the quest for meaning and purpose in life.

What every existentialist (theist or atheist) eventually discovers is this: an understanding of the brevity of life demands that we live it intentionally, assessing our priorities and then allowing them to determine how we'll spend our time. Scripture is full of a kind of existential rhetoric that encourages us to live purposefully and strategically.

King Solomon, writing in Ecclesiastes, said, "In the morning sow your seed, / And in the evening do not withhold your hand; / For you do not know which will prosper, / Either this or that, / Or whether both alike will be good" (Eccl. 11:6 NKJV). In the New Testament, the apostle Paul wrote, "So be very careful how you live. Do not live like those who are not wise, but live wisely. Use every chance you have for doing good, because these are evil times" (Ephesians 5:15–16 NCV).

> *If we do not consciously establish and intentionally pursue what's important and make it our priority, then we forfeit our power to make wise decisions, and we allow our actions to be dictated by others or even by circumstances.*

If we do not consciously establish and intentionally pursue what's important and make it our priority, then we forfeit our power to make wise decisions, and we allow our actions to be dictated by others or even by circumstances. That's no way to live!

Instead, our worldview should shape our priorities. What's a worldview, you might ask? It's a system of beliefs or concepts that help us make sense of the world around us. Ed Young wrote, "Having a consistent worldview is almost like having a pair of eyeglasses with lenses cut and ground just for us. It enables us to see life more clearly and to perceive with accuracy the things around us."

Ultimately our worldview should dictate our priorities. When it doesn't, life becomes frustratingly out of focus and chaotic. What we do, and not just what we say, demonstrates what we believe. If I wanted to understand your worldview, the most revealing thing I could do would be to examine your checkbook and/or your Palm Pilot. A quick look at one or both would be a strong indication of your worldview and your priorities.

Does this sound too simple, or too harsh? It's not. Listen, there are many possible pursuits in life. Some of them are important; some are trivial. Some have lasting impact; some are fleeting. But how we live is a strong indicator of where our true priorities lie: not the ones we speak and espouse to others, the ones we really *act upon*. We must regularly consider whether the things we are involved in are the *best* things, things with long-term or eternal impact—and whether they are a reflection of what we truly believe. After all, we want our actions to be consistent with what we believe, don't we?

Most of our choices are not necessarily wrong or bad ones. They're just not the best ones. And we must recognize that we have an amazing ability to justify every single one of them. The question is not whether the things we do are important; it's whether they are essential. The man or woman who lives life intentionally with well-established priorities is able to distinguish between the important and the essential. And we want you to be just that kind of intentional man or woman.

What's Essential, and What's Not?

We can virtually guarantee that some (if not most) of the things you are involved in are nonessential. How can we make such a bold statement? By virtue of the fact that we live in a culture that is relentlessly moving, constantly demanding, and subtly (and not-so-subtly) encouraging overindulgence and overinvolvement.

You probably didn't mean to set aside what you knew to be most important (we didn't either) and give in to the demands and pressures of the culture, but you've very likely done so in many, many ways. The flood of information and choices coming at us daily virtually demands that we be proactive in sorting through them. If we're passive, we're almost sure to get carried away in the current!

What kinds of nonessential things am I speaking of? I hesitate to get too specific because I want to encourage the kind of serious self-examination that leads to personal inventory taking, not just a reactive legalism. But to give you a little jump start, consider that according to "U.S. Entertainment Industry: 2004 MPA Market Statistics," the average American spends 10.3 hours per day on the following:

- Broadcast television
- Broadcast and satellite radio
- Daily newspapers
- Consumer magazines
- Cable and satellite television
- Box office
- Home video
- Interactive television
- Recorded music
- Video games
- Consumer Internet
- Consumer books

This is solely media consumption and doesn't even take into account the number of hours we spend on other nonessentials, such as home decorating and improvement, shopping, and spectator sports. Now, we aren't against spectator sports but, good grief, what's with the utter obsession? You could literally devote several days to one particular game what with all the pregame shows and hype. Then you have the actual game itself, followed by postgame highlights, stats, and other related news. As if that's not overkill, then you have the next several days devoted to radio/talk show discussions and Internet trivia and analysis. Remember, life is short; do you really want to invest large chunks of time watching other people play games? Get off your duff and get caught up in the things that are going to matter! (Whoops, got a little carried away.)

Perhaps this seems quite obvious. Let me give a personal example of something that may be a bit more subtle.

A few years ago I was invited to serve on a committee for a very worthwhile nonprofit organization. I was told the commitment would require no more than two hours per week, and I reasoned that I surely had that much time to spend for such a good cause. What I *didn't* consider was the drive time, preparation time, and outside work associated with those two hours each week. Most importantly, I didn't consider that, at the time, I had small children with very real and distinct needs.

In total, I spent nearly twenty-five hours a month directly or indirectly involved with this committee. In retrospect, I am certain that the involvement was nonessential for me, especially in that season of my life. I had other priorities that should have taken precedence. Other people could (and should) have filled my position, devoting more energy and focus to it than I was able to provide; no one else could fill my role at home. My family is my priority, but you couldn't tell from my actions. I was overinvolved in a non-essential—and you probably are too.

So try this: write down your activities and responsibilities for a week. All of them. Now rank or sort them into three categories: essential, nonessential, and trivial. Not sure what distinguishes between the essential, nonessential, and the trivial? Think of it this way: if a water pipe bursts in your home, having it repaired immediately is essential, right? Water can damage Sheetrock, carpet, and the furnishings, and your water supply will have to be cut off until the pipe is repaired. Since running water is pretty important to most of us, immediate repair would be essential. But if the kitchen faucet is dripping, you would probably classify the drip as a nonessential. Sure, it may be annoying, but it won't likely hurt anything if you leave it for later. If the same faucet is working just fine but water spots are on it, unless you're a complete neat freak, you'll probably say that the wiping of the water spots is trivial. It's not the kind of thing that's going to stop you dead in your tracks.

Take a look at the list you just made. Does it reflect your priorities? If it doesn't, begin by eliminating the trivial and seeking ways to cut out at least 50 percent of those things you ranked nonessential. Be ruthless. This is your life, your time, your responsibility. No one can do this but you. You're going to want to thank me, but don't waste your time. That letter would fit into the nonessential category!

TIME AND CONTENTMENT

Many of our priorities are out of order, and we don't live intentionally because we operate out of the *perception of lack*. In other words, our actions are dictated not by what we believe, but by what we believe we *lack*. Some people believe they don't have enough time. Have you ever heard someone say, "I'd like to do that, but I just don't have as much time as other people do"? That's hilarious! The person who uses this excuse for failing to live intentionally is implying that somewhere out there are other people who manage to enjoy more than twenty-four hours in every day!

That idea is completely flawed. Time is no respecter of persons. We all have the same twenty-four-hour span in which to operate.

Presidents have it. CEOs have it. Musicians and bakers and postal carriers have it. Mother Teresa had twenty-four hours in every day. So did Leonardo da Vinci and Martin Luther King. How did the men and women who made significant impact on our world do so with only twenty-four-hour increments of time at their disposal? The answer is simple: they respected the rhythms of work and rest, and they learned to prioritize the time they had.

Dwight D. Eisenhower, the thirty-fourth president of the United States, summed it up this way: "The older I get the more wisdom I find in the ancient rule of taking first things first; a process which often reduces the most complex human problem to a manageable proportion." Similarly, C. S. Lewis instructed that we can only truly enjoy "second," or nonessential, things by placing the essential things first. If we lose focus on first things and pursue second things as *if* they were first, he said, we will lose both.

> *The secret to living an intentional life is in large part associated with developing an attitude of contentment.*

Instead of using our modern time-saving devices to allow us to add yet more nonessential things to our calendars, why couldn't we use them to gain more time for essentials *and* for soul rest? We recommend eliminating some of the trivial forms of activity and entertainment, television viewing, and shopping, and instead prioritizing your time so that what matters most consistently appears at the top of your to-do list.

Virtually all of us wish we had more time; too many of us also wish we had more stuff. Someone once asked multibillionaire Nelson Rockefeller how much money it would take to satisfy him, and his reported response was "Just a little bit more!" Can't you relate? Maybe you thought you'd be satisfied with just one DVD player or casting rod or high-powered driver, but you really just meant one *more*. Maybe just having one pair of ridiculously expensive shoes or jeans seemed as if it would satisfy you, but what you've discovered is that you lust for one *more*.

The secret to living an intentional life is in large part associated with developing an attitude of contentment. Note that I say "developing." We are not born with contentment; we're born grasping! You'd think Adam and Eve would have been incredibly content. They enjoyed uninterrupted communion with God, a lush garden, plenty of good food to eat, and limitless beauty to behold. But in spite of this, they were not content and lusted after the one thing they felt God had denied them. We're not born content, but we can *learn* contentment. The apostle Paul wrote that he had *learned* to be content in every circumstance, whether he had a lot or only a little (Philippians 4:11–12). We can learn it too.

One way to learn contentment is to be actively thankful for what we already have. When was the last time you deliberately fixed your mind on the things God has already blessed you with? If your answer was honest (and anything like ours), that's too long! The truth is, the most valuable, rewarding, precious, beautiful, and fulfilling things in life are intangible and don't cost us a dime.

My (Sam) family has a ranch in the hill country about an hour from Austin, Texas. Our family loves to go out there on the weekends because it is a great place to retreat and find solace in God's creation. Several years ago, there was some discussion about putting in a swimming pool that could enhance our enjoyment and would offer great fellowship for the extended family and cousins. In this age of "more is better" and "more makes us happier," I was surprised and a little disappointed when my parents (with eight grandchildren) felt it would be an unnecessary luxury; no one lived on the ranch, and it wasn't used enough to warrant a pool, much less the upkeep it would require.

The most interesting thing happened: my children and I began to actually explore the ranch's creek and its surroundings. We cleared most of the cedar trees and brush and put up a hammock and swing and found a spot for a picnic table. I made a pit, lined it with limestone for fire, and began cooking hot dogs and s'mores. I played my guitar, everybody sang, and the girls danced.

We started having more rain than usual, so the creek was full more of the time than previously. In fact, natural springs started flowing again from the sides of the creek, and we even built a dam. This is where my kids spend all of their time from sunup to sundown, swimming and using their imaginations and creativity with games of adventure and exploration. Need I say more?

We need to be more than just aware of these things; we need to be intentionally, actively, and continually appreciative of them. Thank God for your health. Thank Him for hot water when you need to shower, and for cold water when you're thirsty. Thank Him for shelter and clothing and food, and for the beauty of the sunrise and the sunset. Thank Him for ocean waves and treetops, for friendships and family relationships. When you do this, you will strengthen your priorities and learn to focus on what matters most. Calvin Miller said, "If the little things like oxygen and oatmeal remind you of God's goodness and turn your anthems Godward, then the material blessings of God will have a noble purpose."

A related principle is to consider all the things in our lives as gifts from God and signs that point us to Him. In his excellent book *The God Who Loves You*, Peter Kreeft recommended that we conceptualize the whole world as a love letter from God. Try this for just one hour and see if it doesn't make a radical difference for you: See the sunrise not just as a mindless mechanical necessity but as God's smile. See a wave not just as tons of cold saltwater crashing down on the shore but as God's playful action. Keep in mind, Kreeft said, that this is not merely some mind game or psychological trick: this is reality. He went on to suggest that we see a leaf on every tree as a work of art made by the divine Artist with the intention that we notice it, know it, love it, rejoice in it. We challenge you to try this out and see what it does for your contentment, not to mention your sense of joy and appreciation for being alive.

Another powerful exercise in contentment includes the art of living in the moment. Need some help on this? Take a look at this meditation from Saint Augustine's *Prayer Book*. This was his morning prayer:

Just for Today

Lord, for tomorrow and its needs, I do not pray;
Keep me, my God, from stain and sin,
Just for today.

Let me both diligently work and duly pray.
Let me be kind in word and deed,
Just for today.

Let me be slow to do my will, prompt to obey;
Help me to sacrifice myself,
Just for today.

And if today my tide of life should ebb away;
Give me thy Sacraments divine,
Sweet Lord, today.

So for tomorrow and its need I do not pray,
But keep me, guide me, love me, Lord,
Just for today.

THE POWER OF ONE

Besides altering our perception of time and focusing on what causes true contentment, we'd like to introduce four powerful concepts we've found invaluable in establishing and keeping our priorities in order. The first is called "the power of one." Søren Kierkegaard, the Danish philosopher and father of Christian existentialism, wrote that "purity of heart is to will one thing." There is power, Kierkegaard argued, in focusing on one good thing (God) to the exclusion of everything else. When we have that kind of purity or simplicity of heart, we truly *can* experience peace and simplicity in a fast-paced world.

I (Sam) learned Kierkegaard's *power of one* theory in a way I will never forget. From the time my wife's water broke in March of 1991, I was a man with one mission: to get her to the labor-and-delivery room of the hospital so that our daughter could be safely born. It was our first experience with pregnancy and childbirth, and in my world, absolutely nothing took precedence over ensuring a safe delivery. Everything else—and I do mean everything—took a backseat.

No amount of money could have lured me away from my mission, no form of entertainment could have distracted me, and no other person could have competed for my time and attention in those precious hours. I mean this literally when I say that nothing in heaven or on earth (short of death itself) could have kept me from my assignment or diverted my *one thing* focus. When my wife's labor pains began, life suddenly became incredibly clear: one thing mattered, and one thing only.

Perhaps you can relate. Maybe you've had a doctor's appointment that crystallized things for you, or a work deadline so important that secondary things fell completely off your radar. Surely you can remember a time when you were so focused on one thing that everything else paled in comparison. Just as circumstances can force us into a *one thing* focus, we can also *choose* to focus on one thing. Whatever the catalyst, in order to live intentional lives, we must boil it all down to one thing ultimately.

What will your one thing be? Take a look at what author and pastor Chuck Swindoll said about it: "When Christ becomes our central focus—our reason for existence—contentment replaces our anxiety as well as our fears and insecurities." When our one focus is established, Swindoll insisted, we can live the rest of our lives in that surety:

> If you live in light of Christ's return each day of your life, it does wonders for your perspective . . . It also makes you recognize how many needless activities we get involved in on this earth. Sort of like rearranging the deck chairs on the *Titanic*. Don't bother! Don't get lost in the insignificant details. He's coming soon. Recognize the urgency and the simplicity of the hour.

Can we afford to have any other focus? We don't think so.

The Power of Disowning

It is a basic spiritual law that the more you give away, the more freedom you will enjoy. There is power in disowning, in divesting ourselves of the things we've accumulated in life that weigh us down and keep us bound. Generally speaking, a distinct correlation exists between the amount of money or possessions we have and our ensuing level of anxiety and sense of burden. You've heard the saying "Less is more"? Listen, it really is. Simplicity equals freedom. The less stuff you have, the less you actually have to worry about. German theologian Dietrich Bonhoeffer said, "Earthly possessions dazzle our eyes and delude us into thinking that they can provide security and freedom from anxiety. If our hearts are set upon them, our reward is an anxiety whose burden is intolerable."

Richard Foster said that anything we own that we can't afford to part with really owns us! I wonder what's owning you that you could disown for the sake of peace and simplicity. How could you get rid of the excess stuff that you've accumulated in a way that pleases God and helps someone else? Do you have the courage to let go of your pursuit of materialism? What could you disown today that would help you to clean up or throw out the materialistic influences in your life? Are you brave enough to try?

Luke 3:10–11 gives some practical instruction from John the Baptist: "So the people asked him, saying, 'What shall we do then?' He answered and said to them, 'He who has two tunics, let him give to him who has none; and he who has food, let him do likewise'" (NKJV). Needless to say, most of us in this affluent society have two of many things: we live in excess and overindulgence. We can afford to give away what we do not need. And when we do, we are free to focus more fully on what we need most.

THE POWER OF NO

Perhaps the most delicious word in all the English language is *yes*. We like to say it, and we love to hear it. There is something very powerful, even exhilarating, about this affirmative word. Our American culture has us believing that we can (and should) have it all. But it has neglected to tell us the cost. "Yes, you can own this new, loaded-out car, the cost of which would feed a family of four on the African continent for several years." (And for six hundred dollars a month for thirty-six months at 18 percent interest, it's all yours, Baby!) "Yes, you can have the promotion and the corner office, even though it means you'll see even less of your family than you do now."

> *Saying no is perhaps the single most empowering thing you can do to take control of your time and your life, and it is essential if you're going to move your priorities to where they should be and keep them there.*

The next time you're tempted to say yes, remember that you have another powerful word in your arsenal of language: *no*. Saying no is perhaps the single most empowering thing you can do to take control of your time and your life, and it is essential if you're going to move your priorities to where they should be and keep them there. Here are some useful ideas to practice the power of no.

USE IT OR LOSE IT: EXERCISE YOUR *No* MUSCLE

The best way to learn to say no is to start saying it often, and with confidence—even if you don't feel confident at first. Saying no is easier if you feel that you are worthy and valuable, that you matter and your needs are important. Unless you do, you will be tempted to defer to others and to allow them to dictate your life, your schedule, and your priorities. The extent to which you are able to see yourself as valuable will empower you to begin drawing firm lines and saying no when you need to.

Just Say No with No Explanation

When someone confronts with an opportunity, it is perfectly all right to say no without offering a lengthy explanation as to why. You can be polite in doing so, but you need not explain or justify your decision unless you wish to. Many times we justify our no's so that people will still like us (which is what we so often hope they will do when we say yes). If you do offer a lengthy explanation, nine times out of ten you can count on the other person finding a way around your conflict in order for you to say yes, and you're back to zero.

Another good reason to be wary of giving explanations is that oftentimes in the process of explaining why you can't do something, you fortify your reasons for doing it, and sometimes the other person may even forget that you initially said no. People may act incredulous at a simple, unqualified *no*, but that doesn't mean you have to keep talking. Don't be afraid to let the chips fall where they may.

Remember, you live before an audience of One—His opinion is the one that matters; let that One guide your yes's and no's, and make yourself accountable first, last, and always to Him. This may be very difficult at first, but let me assure you, you can do it! Go ahead. Give it a try. Just say no. Then stop talking.

START WITH "PROBABLY NOT"

Another great way to say no is to say something like: "I will probably not be able to do that, but let me check the family calendar." This does two things: first, it allows you to make no (and not yes) your default answer. Second, it allows you to reconsider or to take a longer time to consider requests that you may later deem worthy.

There was a season in the life of my (Sam) family when we sorely needed to rein in our schedules. (There are six of us.) So we made a pact as a family that if any opportunity came up for activity or involvement, we would defer the decision to the family as a whole. This proved to be an extremely effective way to be more diligent (and prayerful) about our decisions and choices. I highly recommend it. The practice of seeking God's wisdom and direction, as well as our family's, on even small things only strengthened our faith as a family and developed our prayer life in a powerful way.

SAY, "LET ME SLEEP ON IT"

This is another great strategy that says no matter what the decision, you will not make it immediately but will allow some time to pass as you chew on it for a while. Always, always try to buy some time. This tactic defuses the lure of the emotional appeal and affords you the objectivity you need to discern whether the opportunity is in keeping with your priorities and values. It also creates some space into which God can speak and you can listen. Rarely should you make a decision or commitment on the spot, particularly because it is *your* time and *your* energy that will be required.

THE POWER OF BOUNDARIES

Any commitment we make to a program, a person, a task, or an obligation costs us something. At the very least, saying yes to one thing may (and very likely will) mean saying no to something else. Every yes—whether it's to join a committee, try out for a team, volunteer for a worthy project, or agree to a date with someone special—has costs associated with it. They may be costs we have considered and are quite willing to pay, or there may be hidden and unwanted costs. We must understand that not only is our time limited and precious, but we have a limited reservoir of physical, emotional, social, and spiritual reserves too. It is our responsibility to consider the costs of each decision we make, or face the consequence of depletion if we do not.

> *The truth is, being an extreme people-pleaser is pure selfishness at its core because the motive is to be liked and affirmed, not to truly serve for another's benefit.*

The solution is really quite simple. We need to move in our boundaries. We can still say yes to good things; we just need to say yes less often if we find ourselves being drained. Boundaries define us and reinforce the notion that we are separate and distinct from others. Boundaries inform others what we like and don't like, what we will accept and will not accept, what we can tolerate and cannot tolerate. They're good. They're useful. In fact, they're essential. People with no boundaries have no lives or, at the very least, no clear priorities.

As a counselor I can tell you that many, many people struggle in the area of boundaries. Someone once suggested to me that a counselor could establish a full-time job of writing books exclusively on this topic and live off the royalties for the rest of his or her life. (I wonder if that's been done yet?!) Anyway, the point is that the need is tremendous. Christians are not immune to boundary problems. In fact, they may be more susceptible because they often can confuse their unhealthy people-pleasing tendencies with the idea of selflessness. But the truth is, being an extreme people-pleaser is pure selfishness at its core because the motive is to be liked and affirmed, not to truly serve for another's benefit. As a result, the people-pleaser is scattered and is not slowing down long enough to be truly productive for the kingdom. When the opinions of others instead of God's guidance dictate our actions, we're bound for not only physical and mental exhaustion but also spiritual stagnation. For this reason, it's essential that we realize we are 100 percent accountable for the choices we make, and that we have the ability (no, the *responsibility*) to say no when it is required.

There's a misconception afoot that boundaries are walls that keep others out and lead to isolation. They are not. Boundaries are protective and enabling; they protect us from what would rob us of our time and energy, and they enable us to focus on those things that matter most. As such, they are a powerful means of making sure we live according to our priorities.

But the establishment and keeping of boundaries is not easy. It requires us to be assertive and proactive: to know how, when, and why to say no. Let's look at the principal areas where we should establish boundaries, and ways in which we can constructively do so.

BOUNDARIES AROUND THE FAMILY

It is a little clichéd but 100 percent accurate that no one on his deathbed regrets not having spent more time at the office, in front of the television, or on the golf course. Almost everyone with time to reflect upon it, however, regrets not spending more time with his loved ones. Nearly everyone *says* his family is important to him, but not everyone acts upon that conviction.

If your life and your daily decisions do not reflect this value, you are the only one who can do something about the discrepancy. Carve out specific, sacred family time and allow no interruptions. (A rare opening for a tee time at your favorite club is not—I repeat not—an emergency, unless it's at Augusta National or Pebble Beach!) I know of families that devote their entire weekends to family time, unplugging telephones, computers, and televisions so that they may focus exclusively on one another. If this idea makes you nervous, perhaps you should consider that a good reason to give it a try!

BOUNDARIES AROUND YOUR CLOSEST FRIENDSHIPS

Discerning how and when you limit your relationships is difficult—no doubt. As humans, we live within the context of relationship, and we are designed to cultivate and nurture friendships on all levels. Additionally, as Christians, we have a calling to others: God's children primarily manifest His love to the world. So we have a responsibility to seek out others and share God's acceptance and love.

This, however, should not preclude our other responsibilities. We must have limitations or relationship boundaries. Consider Jesus, again, as our example. He chose twelve disciples, and He was very particular, even exclusive, in His purposes. As if that weren't enough, within the group of twelve He chose three—Peter, James, and John—to represent His inner circle of more intimate relationships. Likewise, I think it would be very much like Christ to evaluate whether or not you have spread yourself too thin in the relational arena.

BOUNDARIES AROUND YOUR WORSHIP

Have you ever been to a rock concert and observed people standing on their chairs, waving their arms in the air, shouting at the top of their lungs, or lifting high their illuminated cell phones or cigarette lighters? Then you've observed worship. That's right: the object of the worship was not God, but it was worship just the same. Worship is one of the most unselfconscious impulses in the human heart. We *want* to worship, and we *will* worship. The question is not *if,* it is *how* and *whom* and *when.* If we are not worshiping God, we will almost certainly be worshiping something (or someone) else: a sports hero, a relationship, sex, money, food, pleasure. Something will take His place as the object of our worship.

Nothing pleases God more than when His people worship Him in spirit and in truth. I don't know about you, but when I am enraptured by the beauty of God in true worship, I experience His pleasure and a deep, deep sense of satisfaction. For this reason, I am very careful to guard against anything or anyone that would intrude on this precious and sacred practice. Keep the boundaries around your worship strong. You will be glad you did.

BOUNDARIES AROUND THE SABBATH

We've already written at length about the Sabbath. As we indicated, God created it for us, not for Himself. When we believe this and accept and enjoy this wonderful gift from our loving Father, we are helped and healed. Our souls have room to breathe. But we cannot wait until we feel like protecting the Sabbath with boundaries; it is a decision that we must make in advance. When we preestablish the importance of observing the Sabbath by drawing firm lines around it, we honor it, and we are honored by it.

Honor the Sabbath by keeping it set apart for you and for your family. Slow down, unplug, and refuse to schedule anything during this time. It is, after all, a matter of obedience to remember the Sabbath and keep it holy.

BOUNDARIES AROUND YOUR MIND AND HEART

Do you know who is the ultimate sentry determining what comes into your mind and heart? You are! We often act like victims or innocent bystanders whose minds are somehow filled with images and information we do not want. If it came in, we let it in! You and I should be ever vigilant and unapologetically intolerant about the onslaught of filth that we're bombarded with day in and day out. Proverbs warns, "Be careful what you think, because your thoughts run your life" (4:23 NCV).

This little nugget says it all. What finds space in your head will eventually find space in your heart. And what finds space in your heart, and in mine, will eventually be evidenced in our behavior and our words. The vile and worthless stuff we're exposed to routinely is like sewage that seeps into the ground and eventually pollutes the water we drink. It's disgusting. It's lethal. And we can proactively fence it out by setting limits and being diligent to maintain them. The boundary around our minds and hearts is one we simply cannot ignore or allow to become run-down. If you have allowed this, perhaps it's time for some serious fence building in your life.

BOUNDARIES AROUND YOUR FREE TIME

We have more options today to fill our leisure time than did any generation in history. For that very reason, we must be diligent in drawing some lines around that time and deciding how we will and won't spend it. Unfortunately, many of us leave our free time to chance, allowing whatever comes along to fill it. Free time is meant to provide soul rest, not confusion or exhaustion or distraction. Let's keep in mind that soul rest doesn't always have to be a serious endeavor.

> *Be as intentional about free time as you are about work time or worship time or family time. It matters.*

Be as intentional about free time as you are about work time or worship time or family time. It matters. When you consider how to spend your free time, ask yourself, *Is this good, true, beautiful, and profitable? Will it make me stronger? Deeper? Fuller? More free?* Let the answers help you establish boundaries around your free time.

BOUNDARIES AROUND YOUR PURPOSE

Your life is no accident. God created you with a special purpose and mission to fulfill. Others may try to dictate that mission to you or to enlist you in the fulfillment of *their* mission to the exclusion of your own. But it is your responsibility to keep God's plans for you front and center and to weigh all requests, opportunities, and agendas against them.

Philosophers through the ages have asked, "What is the meaning of life?" Perhaps the question we should be asking instead is, "God, what is the meaning of *my* life?" His Word assures us that He has a purpose: "'I know the plans that I have for you,' declares the LORD, 'plans for welfare and not for calamity to give you a future and a hope'" (Jeremiah 29:11 NASB). It is up to us to seek and to fulfill God's purposes for our own lives. And when we see and understand those purposes, it is our responsibility to guard them carefully and to measure everything else we might choose against them.

Determine your God-directed meaning and focus, and order your life around it. Don't let other things or people intrude across those boundaries. Guard it as if it were treasure, and live it daily.

One Final Word on Priorities

In many ways what we are asking you to do is simple. But we don't for a minute believe that it's easy. We're not promoting a series of strategies, tips, or techniques that you might expect from a time-management solution. Oh, sure, if you want to practice specific, measurable goal setting and learn to delegate responsibilities, that is great. But what we are emphasizing instead has more to do with the attitude and inclination of your heart.

In light of your brief time here on earth, decide now to determine your true priorities and to live by them. That's the heart and soul of it. Have the confidence to reject the trivial (and much of the nonessential). Learn to say no. Slow down and feel the true rhythm and cadence of life, called by the One who knows you by name. Listen to His voice and the cry of your own heart. Then do whatever it takes to follow Him, fully, freely, and without hindrance, even when it means going against the tide of the world.

What If . . .

. . . you took ownership of your time and your schedule and laid claim to the power of *no*?

. . . you opened your physical and spiritual eyes and really took in the beauty and glory of God's creation?

. . . you truly felt content with the way you spent your time?

EIGHT

Move Away from Technology

None but those who have experienced them can
conceive of the enticements of science.
—Mary Shelley

Whether you lived as a minister or a murderer, odds are good that at your funeral, someone would recite the twenty-third Psalm. Why? Because this psalm contains some of the most comforting words ever penned: "The LORD is my shepherd, I shall not want" (v. 1). In the twenty-first century, however, we have a new psalm of comfort. It goes like this:

Technology is my shepherd; I shall not want.
It makes me lie down in front of the high-definition screen.
It leads me with incessant noise.
It makes me feel significant.
Though I walk through the valley of no cell-phone coverage,

(Can you hear me now?) you are with me.

My Blackberry, my laptop, they comfort me.

You set wireless access before me in the presence of my family.

You anoint my head with Bluetooth; my e-mail overflows.

Surely Microsoft and Verizon will follow me all the days of
    my life

And I will dwell in the database forever (unless I am
    inadvertently deleted).

The point is that technology has become godlike in our culture. Daily we bow down at its altar and give it homage, not realizing that by buying in to its power, we have sold our souls for a lie. Has more and more technology really made our lives easier, as it promises to do? Sure, there are many wonderful ways technology has enhanced the quality of life in the Western world, but what have we sacrificed for it?

Cultural prophet and late NYU professor Neil Postman wrote two watershed books dealing with the advent and pervasiveness of technology. In one of them, *Technopoly,* Postman revealed how devout technology's disciples have become: "Technopoly is a state of culture. It is also a state of mind. It consists in the deification of technology, which means that the culture seeks its authorization in technology, finds its satisfaction in technology, and takes its orders from technology."

Technology is virtually impossible to escape. Go to the park for a jog, and you'll encounter other joggers talking on their cell phones or listening to music on their iPods. Get on an airplane, and the flight attendant will recite a litany of all the electronic devices that are permissible for use and when. Try to subscribe to basic cable and prepare to sort through the "bargain" packages of digital cable and satellite television access, offering hundreds of channels, not just a handful.

We Americans strap techno-gadgets to our belts, our ears, and our wrists, giving the appearance that we are ready to either perform in concert with Madonna or walk on the moon—when we're really just going to the store for a gallon of milk! We're connected when we're working in the yard, walking the dog, or even moving from the car to the office and back. In fact, some of us are so "wired" that we rarely speak to the persons immediately around us anymore!

At dinner the other night I saw a man who was supposedly having dinner with his wife and two kids (family man), talking on his cell (businessman), feeding his baby a bottle (nurturing father), and drinking a glass of red wine (trying to "relax")—all at the same time! Quite a phenomenon!

THE NEW MONSTER ON THE BLOCK

Mary Wollstonecraft Shelley may not be a household name, but you definitely know her work. She wrote a novel about a man who tried to create life from nonlife, whose little experiment turned tragic and led to his ultimate demise. The man's name was Frankenstein, or "Frahnken-steen" if you're a Gene Wilder fan.

The problem was not with Dr. Frankenstein's creation, per se, but with his negligence toward the monster he created. Though fiction, this story shows us the reality of how frightening thoughtlessly managed technology can be. Technology in and of itself is not the problem; rather, it is our inability to keep it harnessed that threatens to master us—instead of the reverse.

Mary Shelley subtitled her novel "The Modern Prometheus." If you remember your Greek mythology, Prometheus was a man who stole fire from the gods to help better the lives of his fellow men, believing that fire would enable them to forge tools as well as warm themselves. The gods punished Prometheus despite his noble intentions, chaining him to a rock where an eagle plucked at his liver every single day. The moral of the story? Only gods, not mere mortals, could handle fire.

Postmodern man knows that fire has helped him. No argument there. But when fire surges beyond the realm of our control, the results can be disastrous. You may want to grill a steak on the Jennaire, but you don't want a raging fire in your kitchen. You might like a fireplace in your bedroom, but you don't want to burn your bed. You may use the heater to warm your car on a frosty morning, but you'd prefer *not* to see smoke coming from beneath its hood! When fire rages out of control, people suffer.

Shelley was prophetically ahead of her time when she warned against abusing the power that comes with increased knowledge—and technology is indeed "increased knowledge." Movies such as *Jurassic Park, War Games,* and *I, Robot* echo this techno-gone-wrong theme. Have we, like poor Victor Frankenstein, created a monster we can no longer control?

Sure, we can clone a sheep, but we can also harness enough nuclear power to blow ourselves up three times over. Yes, the Internet puts a host of enticing factoids at our fingertips, from the early history of Outer Mongolia to the subject of the Beatles' song "Hey Jude." (We'll save you the Google time: it was written for John Lennon's son, Julian.) But the World Wide Web can also help an anarchist blow up a federal building in Oklahoma City, teach Al-Qaeda terrorists to use commercial airplanes as deadly missiles, or lead a sexual predator directly to your doorstep.

The problem with this monster we call "technology" is that no one is really taking a serious look at its ugly underbelly—and not just these few frightening things we've mentioned. Smaller, subtler threats exist as well. The gadgets we loved have awed us with their speed, clever noises, and instant images, and we have been all too ready to believe that they will improve our lives, help us make more money, and give us more time to spend with those we love.

Now, if a protest is forming on your lips, do not put this book down yet. We're not kidding: this chapter may save your life. We are not antitechnology Luddites. I am writing these words on a Dell Inspiron laptop, with my Motorola cell phone and Blackberry nearby. We are not going to ask you to go Bohemian and toss your toys out the window—though that might be therapeutic for some. What we *are* going to do is ask you to go Socratic. In other words, start living the examined life by asking yourselves a few probing questions.

Are You Controlling Technology, or Is It Controlling You?

Jeff "You-might-be-a-redneck-if" Foxworthy might be one of the most hilarious guys around. He has all kinds of audiences in stitches with his redneck-if humor. He asks his audience to examine themselves with lines like, "You might be a redneck if your porch caves in and injures more than four dogs," or "You might be a redneck if you go to a family reunion to find a date." Let's apply the Foxworthy method to technology and suggest a few tests of our own:

- You might be controlled by technology if, after you drive home from work, you sit in your garage talking on your cell phone to squeeze in one more call before you greet the family.

- You might be controlled by technology if your television gets over thirty channels.
- You might be controlled by technology if you bring your cell, Blackberry, or laptop with you on vacation (or to lunch!).
- You might be controlled by technology if you check your e-mail at home more than three times a day.
- You might be controlled by technology if, when you are seated in church listening to the pastor's sermon, your cell phone rings and you take the call. (And yes, I've seen it happen!)

It's amazing how we allow these time-saving devices to intrude upon our personal time. Take the telephone, for instance. Some people feel utterly obligated to answer the phone every time it rings. It never occurs to them that they have the option not to: they can let the call go to voice mail instead. (It also never occurs to some that they can turn off their answering machines or voice mail.) Are things really as urgent as we make them out to be? Of course there are extenuating circumstances. We know that. But really—how important is it that you tell your best friend what you just bought at the grocery store, or what the highlight was from last night's Rockets game?

So we ask you: Can you go a day without checking your personal e-mail account? Could you turn your home phone off for an entire day? Could you refrain from watching your favorite news broadcast or reality television series for one evening? Have you ever tried driving in silence, even if your radio, CD player, or DVD player is working properly? Do you shudder at the thought of leaving the house without your cell phone? If you cannot fathom doing any of these things, then you might be controlled by technology.

Is Technology Bringing a Sense of Peace and Well-Being to Your Life?

Think about it for a moment: Are your techno-toys bringing you the joy you are searching for? Do you have more peace in your life because you have a cell phone strapped to your waist or tucked in your purse? Are you sleeping better because you can now receive e-mails anytime and anyplace from anyone—even those people you don't particularly want to hear from? Do you enjoy feeling obligated to reply to the steady stream of unsolicited messages you are receiving?

Do you have more simplicity in your life because you have an awesome CD, MP3, or DVD player? How about that satellite TV: Do all the programming options and channels give you a deep sense of satisfaction? Has the Xbox significantly enhanced your child's social development? If technology is not "showing you the love," then have you decided to stop being dependent upon it?

> *Think about it for a moment: Are your techno-toys bringing you the joy you are searching for? Do you have more peace in your life because you have a cell phone strapped to your waist or tucked in your purse?*

If you can't answer yes to these questions, but you persist in looking to your "toys" for peace and well-being, we suggest you try to figure out why.

Is Technology Deepening Your Relationships with Others and with God?

Almost every Sunday I stand at the door of the church, greeting people as they leave the worship service. Before they hit the exits, many of them are already firing up their cell phones to check their messages. Wouldn't that time be better spent talking with those around them or perhaps seeking out someone new and doing all they can to make that person feel welcome and at home? We rarely speak to passersby anymore; we're too plugged in to notice those we pass, much less look them in the eye! How can we ever hope to love our neighbors when we are completely distracted or unaware in their presence?

We realize this is harsh stuff, but it's time for us to get authentic before God. Has your home computer eaten up time you might have spent in God's Word and in prayer? Does your iPod help you to hear His voice? Now that you are exponentially more accessible to others through your phone or smart device, do you find you are more, or less, accessible to God? Is He more, or less, accessible to you? What we really should be asking over and over again is not "Can you hear me now?" but "Can we hear *God* now?"

What's Behind the Constant Buzz?

At times I sit and watch television simply to veg out. I find that when I do, I'm using technology to escape into another story—any story besides my own. Maybe it's the LA Lakers' story, the Middle East story, the latest celebrity story, the Wall Street story, the political debate story, or the latest love story . . . just so long as it's some other story to avoid the dull or harsh realities of my own. Don't we often use the tube as a diversion or to avoid being alone with our thoughts? And we just as easily use the computer too; e-mailing or instant messaging over and over can give us the sense that we are accomplishing something or at least connecting with others.

Quentin J. Schultze, the author of *Habits of the High-Tech Heart,* says incessant messaging, however, doesn't equate to intimacy:

> When we message too much, we begin to lose intimacy
> with others, the natural world, the Creator, and even our-
> selves. Faster messaging can be an instrumental good—
> such as getting stock market quotes more quickly—but it
> is far less likely to be a moral good. Morally conducive forms
> of knowing, such as conversing and contemplating, are slow,
> thoughtful and personal.

In reality, truly knowing someone requires spending actual time together eating, playing, laughing, crying, being silent, and simply experiencing life. (That's why it's so hard to make a long-distance relationship work—but that's another book altogether!)

If we rely on the constant buzz of high-tech toys for escape or relationships, or reassurance or validation of our own significance, we're headed for trouble. The toys can't deliver. They're not meant to. Again, we're not advocating a rejection of all technological progress, but we *are* suggesting that the answer to our deepest needs lies elsewhere. According to Abraham J. Heschel, "The solution to mankind's most vexing problems will not be found in renouncing technical civilization, but in attaining some degree of independence of it. In regard to external gifts, to outward posses-sions, there is only one proper attitude—to have them and to be able to do without them."

We will cease to be controlled by technology and techno-toys when we can live without them. How do we know we can do with-out them? By seeking to balance the appropriating of technology with abstaining from it. In a word: moderation. Listen to what Schultze has to say about it: "Although we can easily see the value of moderation in eating and drinking, we do not recognize the same virtue when it comes to information pursuits. We naively give users of cyber-technologies special protection from charges of avarice or greed."

We may readily admit the dangers of eating too much or getting drunk, but we let our addictions to technology slide under the radar. It's time to wake up and realize that all extremes, save the extreme pursuit of God, are an unsatisfying form of idolatry.

How to Stop Sucking Your High-Tech Thumb

At this point you may be thinking, *All that sounds great, guys, but how do I manage to maintain the kind of moderation you're talking about?* Allow me (Ben) to give you an example. My youngest daughter, Claire, sucks her thumb; in fact, she's hopelessly devoted to her thumb! Like an adult who finds comfort in a bagel and coffee, Claire finds comfort in twirling her blankie up around her mouth and slurping away at her thumb. Because her beloved thumb is attached to her body, we can't simply throw it out like a pacifier, so my wife and I have decided to slowly wean her from it. Since she cannot suck her thumb in kindergarten, we don't have to worry about her indulging her digit addiction during school hours. And we hide her blankie from her during the day when she is not in school to lessen the temptation (although she is pretty sly in finding it).

We can *wean* ourselves from the overuse of technology in the same way: little by little. Trust me, this technology-weaning program is not easy. I know, because I'm in the process of it myself, and I often look for my high-tech blankie and thumb throughout the course of the day. But it can be done. It just requires a new outlook and some self-imposed limits.

For the sake of perspective, consider this: less than fifteen years ago, most of us existed quite contentedly without cell phones, voice mail, e-mail, and instant messaging. As a matter of fact, my friend and coauthor Dr. Sam Adams does not own a cell phone today and rarely, if ever, uses e-mail. Dr. Adams has never subscribed to cable television, either. In case you think he might be some sort of reclusive loner, let me also add that he has a wife and four children and *still* manages to survive quite well without much technological assistance! History and Sam are living proof that you do not have to be plugged in to the techno-matrix to get through the day. People have lived without the toys we have at our disposal for ages—and some rugged individualists still do.

I realize not many of you are going to throw out your cell phones or cancel the cable, but if Sam can do without them completely, surely we can bring our usage into moderation.

Self-imposed limits can also help you break your addiction to your high-tech thumb. Here are some suggestions that may help.

- If possible, remove voice mail from your cell phone. (If people need to leave a message for you, they can be "trained" to do so at work, or at home.)
- Turn off your cell phone when you leave work and keep it off until you return to work again. When it is off, keep it in a place where you won't be tempted to turn it back on.
- Limit the number of programs you watch on television. Limit the number of shows your kids watch too. They're not getting any smarter sitting in front of the tube. (Did you?) If you think this doesn't apply to you, start by logging everything

you and the kids watch for a week. We predict you'll be surprised—and appalled.

- Cancel your subscription (or don't subscribe) to satellite television or digital cable. You'll save money each month *and*
avoid carpal tunnel syndrome from repeatedly mashing the
remote to flip through hundreds of channels.

- Don't feel compelled to respond to nonbusiness e-mails as
soon as you receive them. (Remember how long people used
to wait for a written reply to a letter?) In fact, don't feel compelled to respond to them at all.

- Drive to work (or drive your kids to school) without listening
to the radio or CD player. Instead, try carrying on a conversation with those in your car, or, if you're alone, with God.

Little by little, you can begin to immunize yourself to the lure
of technology. Start small, but start now, and be consistent. If you're
still not compelled to move away from technology, consider this:
the longer you persist in high-tech thumb sucking, the longer it will
take to break your habit, and over-teching will most assuredly rob
you of the peace and simplicity you're after.

Learn to Discern

Perhaps more than anything, we need to start practicing dis-
cernment when it comes to our use of technology. We need to ask
ourselves: *What's really beneficial? What's ultimately edifying? What
truly enhances my relationships with others? What inspires and allows
me to make loving my neighbor a reality? What reinforces my commitment to my church, my community, and my loved ones?*

We'll deal with the concept of community more fully in the next chapter, but before we do, consider this final thought:

We did not create the world or even ourselves; all of it, including life, is a gift. We are obligated to accept this inheritance thankfully and to exercise our wills responsibly over the range of our particular part of God's world. We are to be stewards instead of exploiters, listening caregivers rather than noisy messengers, and suffering servants rather than indifferent technicians. (Schultze)

The reason to move away from technology is to listen: to the voices of the past and religious tradition, and to the voices of others, especially the divine Other. If we don't learn to listen, the joys of this life will pass us by. Listening is humbling; its natural outgrowth is gratitude toward God and responsibility toward our neighbor. We cannot hope to listen well unless we eliminate the unnecessary static of technological overload.

> *I love technology and the advantages it offers me, but it is not my Shepherd. True peace and simplicity come not from technology but from the true Healer and Restorer of our souls.*

Trust me. I love technology and the advantages it offers me, but it is not my Shepherd. True peace and simplicity come not from technology but from the true Healer and Restorer of our souls:

The LORD is my shepherd;
I shall not want.
He makes me to lie down in green pastures;

He leads me beside the still waters.
He restores my soul. (Psalm 23:1–3 NKJV)

What If . . .

. . . you actually went somewhere without your cell phone?

. . . you checked your e-mail only at work and started writing real letters to close friends?

. . . you didn't have to have the latest and greatest time-saving device?

NINE

MOVE INTO COMMUNITY

We are to love our neighbor as our self because our neighbor is included in our self. Where do I leave off and where does my neighbor begin? There is no telling, for we are part of one another.
—MIKE MASON

Lance Armstrong entered 1996 as the number-one ranked cyclist in the world. He rode in the Atlanta Olympic Games but was unable to disguise the fact that he was experiencing excruciating pain. When Armstrong finally consulted a doctor, the news was not good: he had testicular cancer that had spread to other areas of his body. His chances of survival (not of racing again—of *living*) were fifty-fifty at best. It seemed that one of America's most promising young athletes might die before he was able to fully test the limits of his greatness.

Most of you know the rest of the story. Lance Armstrong underwent surgeries, intensive chemotherapy, and a challenging rehabilitation regimen, and he fully recovered from his deadly disease. He also made a pretty decent comeback in 1998 (just two years after his initial diagnosis) by winning one of the sport's most grueling races: the Tour de France. Since that time, this remarkable athlete has won the Tour a record six times in a row. How did he do it?

In 1922 a twelve-year-old Macedonian girl named Agnes felt a strong call from God to spread the love of Christ as a missionary. A few years later she joined a group of Irish nuns who were ministering in India and began her work there, teaching young children. Agnes taught school for nearly twenty years, until she sensed a fresh call from God to live as a servant of the poor in the dirty slums of Calcutta. Soon she became the leader of a fledgling order called the Missionaries of Charity.

Today that order, known as the Society of Missionaries, has spread all over the world, including the former Soviet Union and Eastern European countries. It helps the poorest of the poor in a number of countries in Asia, Africa, and Latin America and undertakes relief work in the wake of natural catastrophes such as floods, epidemics, and famine. The order also has houses in North America, Europe, and Australia, where it takes care of shut-ins, alcoholics, the homeless, and AIDS sufferers. Agnes was just one small and frail woman, but she did indeed spread Christ's love to the least and the lost until her death in 1997. Maybe you've heard of her by another name: most called her Mother Teresa. How did she do it?

Captain David Rozelle was on mission in Iraq in 2003 when he unknowingly entered a minefield. In his book *Back in Action*, he described what happened:

As we began rolling, everything exploded . . . It felt as if I were setting my right foot into soft mud or a sponge. I looked down to see blood and bits of bone squeezing out of the side of my right boot. I gave one big push to dive into the arms of two brave men who ran selflessly into the minefield to save me. That was the last time I ever used my right foot.

Rozelle lost his foot to amputation and returned to the United States for months of rehabilitation and additional surgeries. Post-injury, he passionately devoted himself to a program of running, swimming, and weight lifting—not simply to maintain a fit physique, but to function as well as he might with an artificial limb: "I do it because it's what you need to do to make these prosthetic devices work," he said simply. The screen saver on the thirty-two-year-old soldier's computer is a photo taken after he completed a "half-Iron Man" competition: 1.2 miles swimming, 56 miles biking, and 13.1 miles running. In the photo he is smiling. And standing on one leg.

Then in March 2005, this commander of the Regimental Headquarters and Headquarters Troop of the Third Armored Cavalry Regiment based at Fort Carson, Colorado, did something that no other amputee/soldier has ever done: he returned to serve on the same battlefield that nearly claimed his life. How did he do it? How did these three individuals—Lance Armstrong, Mother Teresa, and Captain David Rozelle—overcome such insurmountable odds? How did they manage their remarkable achievements against cancer, poverty, and devastating injury? The answer is not what you might guess. It wasn't motivation, although each had plenty. It wasn't grit, although certainly they had it. It was something less visible, but just as essential: it was *community*.

They each achieved as individuals, but they achieved within the context of a strong, supportive community. Lance Armstrong had an experienced community of physicians, nurses, and physical therapists that helped him back on his bike. And he raced with a strong team or community of bikers who positioned him to win when he did return. A team of nuns and other workers, now numbering some four thousand worldwide, helped Mother Teresa touch the poor, diseased, and dejected on the streets of Calcutta. She lived within that serving community until the day she died. And a team or community of brave fighting men helped rescue David Rozelle in Iraq; then another team of physicians and fellow soldiers helped restore his mobility and his strength so he could return to the battlefield.

The point is not that these three individuals are perfect role models or that we should pattern our lives after theirs. What we want to point out is simply this: not one of these individuals completed his or her mission alone. Each of them proved that it is possible to have all the courage and ability in the world, but without the support, love, and accountability of others in community, the loftiest goals may still lie just out of reach.

If you've made it this far in *Out of Control*, hopefully you've caught the vision to stand against the pressures and influences of this world, saying no to the insane pace of contemporary life, and yes to the God who offers true peace and rest. You will need that initial determination to change, and you are the only one who can summon it. No one else can decide for you. But once you've decided, you'll need something else: a community of like-minded others to encourage and admonish you along the way.

The old, individualistic American mind-set of pulling yourself up by your own bootstraps simply will not work here (forgive us the cowboy analogy; we're Texans). Too many Christians have bought in to the entrepreneurial spirit of rustic individualism but lost sight of the biblical concept of community in the process.

We applaud you if you've already committed yourself to the practices of Sabbath, solitude, prayer, and meditation. We're thrilled if you've determined to shift your priorities and move away from technology. But it may all be for naught if you do not also purpose to ground yourself strongly in community as you seek to do these things. Why? Because there's power in community—a power many of us have yet to explore.

Check out what King Solomon had to say about the power of community, and the devastating effects of trying to live without it:

I saw a man who had no family,
　　no son or brother.
He always worked hard
　　but was never satisfied with what he had.
He never asked himself, "For whom am I working so hard?
　　Why don't I let myself enjoy life?"
This also is very sad and useless.
Two people are better than one,
　　because they get more done by working together.
If one falls down, the other can help him up.
But it is bad for the person who is alone and falls, because no
　　one is there to help.
If two lie down together, they will be warm, but a person
　　alone will not be warm.
An enemy might defeat one person, but two people together
　　can defend themselves;
A rope that is woven of three strings is hard to break.
(Ecclesiastes 4:8–12 NCV)

If the wisest man in the world valued community this highly, can you afford to ignore its manifold benefits?

THE ULTIMATE COMMUNITY

To understand the true power of community, we must begin with an understanding of the *ultimate* community: God Himself. That's right. God is the ultimate community because He is and has always been a triune God: one God in three distinct persons. These three persons, God the Father, God the Son, and God the Holy Spirit, have forever existed in a replenishing, loving, self-giving relationship, making up the perfect community. God exists within this context of community, fellowship, and relationship. We cannot rightly think of Him apart from it.

> *We live in a lost, fragmented, me-first world, but still we long for oneness, for union. And we long for it because we were made for it!*

Now, we realize that the concept of one God in three persons is a mind bender. It always has been, and it always will be. The idea of a triune God in everlasting community with Himself is beyond our capacity to fully comprehend, but we trust it. We believe it is true. In God, and in God alone, exists the perfect community of love, surrender, diversity, and unity.

Is it any wonder, then, that you and I crave union? If we desire to lose ourselves in something or someone else, it is because we are, in our very nature, reflections of the triune God Himself. We live in a lost, fragmented, me-first world, but still we long for oneness, for union. And we long for it because we were made for it! We crave the connection of community because God made us in the image of the ultimate, the perfect community: God Himself.

If there is power in community (and we believe there is!) it is God's power. He made us to live in that power with Him and with others. So, if we are not living in community, we are not reflecting the God who created us. Instead, we are "nowhere" men and women, living far short of our true identities. All healthy communities draw their origins from the eternal, ultimate, triune community that is God. As we seek to bring order and peace to our out-of-control lives, it is encouraging to know that God the Father, God the Son, and God the Holy Spirit stand ready to join with us to do so.

THE LOCAL COMMUNITY

Under the headship of the ultimate community—God—is the local community, the church. God made the church to be a reflection of His own unity, diversity, and equality. *Ekklesia* is the Greek word for "church," which literally means "called-out ones." God has called us out of our isolation and self-absorption into His local community, the church. From our disjointed, broken lives, He invites us into the unity, peace, fellowship, and love of *His* glorious community.

Like a relay race, the Christian life is a team sport. It is not possible (or advisable) to function as a solo runner, to try to run the race alone. While Christ calls us individually, He addresses us collectively as one body, with each of us playing a vital role. When we come to Christ, we become a member of His body. I don't know what body part you may be. Maybe you're an arm. Or a foot, or an ear. Large or small, obvious or ancillary, each of us has a role to fill as a member of the functional body of Christ.

In his excellent book *Life Together,* Dietrich Bonhoeffer exhorted fellow believers to fully live in community, encouraging one another as members of the same body:

> God has willed that we should seek and find His living Word in the witness of a brother, in the mouth of a man. Therefore, the Christian needs another Christian who speaks God's Word to him. He needs him again and again when he becomes uncertain and discouraged . . . The Christ in his own heart is weaker than the Christ in the word of his brother; his own heart is uncertain, his brother's is sure.

Bonhoeffer was saying what we instinctively know but don't always acknowledge: we're in this thing together, and it's good that we are. We are united, completed, defined, and refined within the context of the local community: the church of the Lord Jesus Christ. In this body there is a place for individuality and distinctiveness, but it is Christ who binds us together in a unity that can—and should!—empower us to impact the world.

In fact, Bonhoeffer went on to say that to deny the local community is to deny the one who made it: "Into the community you were called. The call was not meant for you alone; in the community of the called you bear your cross, you struggle, you pray. If you scorn the fellowship of the brethren, you reject the call of Christ." Now, we realize earlier (see Chapter 5) Bonhoeffer seemed to imply that we must go it alone because we are called "alone." It's simpler than it seems. We alone are responsible in regard to answering the call to believe in Christ and, therefore, be saved—no one can answer that call for us. But for the rest of our lives, once we've answered yes to that initial call, we are exhorted to struggle, to live, to walk out our faith *together* in community. Otherwise, we don't make it.

If we want to develop and maintain the peace and simplicity that run counter to our crazed culture, we will not likely do it outside the local community, the church. At least not for long. Either you and I live as unique members of an interconnected community, experiencing and enjoying the fruit of Christ's life within us, or we live as terrified, demanding, self-absorbed islands, disconnected and reliant on only the finite resources we ourselves

> *Yes, we need solitude for rest and renewal, but we need community for encouragement, accountability, and empowerment.*

can bring. It has rightly been said that "no man is an island." Yes, we need solitude for rest and renewal, but we need community for encouragement, accountability, and empowerment. The local community has a synergy that we can't find anywhere else. The body of Christ is a living, dynamic force, and we need to be connected to it if we hope not simply to survive but to flourish.

THE SUPPORTIVE COMMUNITY

We need the ultimate community: God. We need the local community: the church. And we need the supportive community: a more intimate subset of the local community that will hold our feet to the fire when we falter and struggle against the temptations of the world. Your nuclear family could be a supportive community. Your neighbors, small group, men's or women's prayer group, or your close friends could function as a supportive community. Whatever its makeup, we all need that intimate place "where everybody knows your name." Where we can't hide or be anonymous. Where we can tell the truth, even when it's painful to do so.

I like the story behind Alcoholics Anonymous. I like what it stands for. I like the fact that a guy named Bill knew he needed help and formed a supportive community to meet his need that would later come to be known as AA. Bill found help, then devoted himself to helping others. In the years since, millions of men and women have found freedom from their deadly and debilitating addictions by following the Twelve Steps of Alcoholics Anonymous. Although they are not presented as such, the Twelve Steps are based on biblical principles. (This is why they work, incidentally.) I like that. And I like the humility and accountability found in this supportive community. I sometimes wonder if there isn't more authenticity in many AA meetings than there is in our local churches.

At AA meetings, members introduce themselves by their first names, saying something like this: "My name is Ben, and I'm an alcoholic." Even as I write this, I wonder if you might think I am making some sort of confession related to alcohol. I'm not. That's not my addiction. But I do confess (and should) that I *have* addictions—and so do you.

"Now, wait a minute," you might be saying, "you may have your addictions, but I don't. I'm clean." Hear me out. What I mean to suggest is that each of us has areas of his or her life that can and do quickly career out of control. Habits, issues, *pet sins,* if you will, that continue to hold us captive—either in secret or openly. A while back, I suggested to my men's small group that we implement some AA-style practices. We started each meeting with similar confessional introductions: "Hi, my name is _____, and I'm a _____." We filled in the blank with our particular addiction, such things as greed-aholic, lust-aholic, rage-aholic, control-aholic, golf-acholic, etc. Then we proceeded with the business at hand. It was a brutal, yet strangely healing undertaking.

If we're to break free of our addictions and move toward the things that promote a balanced and healthy life, then we desperately need a supportive community. Please understand that we aren't saying it has to be a formal group. But we are saying that all of us need to surround ourselves with a handful of people who will support our efforts toward peace and simplicity, who will help us slow down to a reasonable pace—and call us on our failure to do so.

Stop and identify the people who might give you the love, support, and accountability you need to make these life-changing movements. Maybe your roommate or your best friend would be glad to do so. Or your spouse or business partner. Perhaps you could gather some like-minded friends from your church or your neighborhood to start a supportive community for those who are feeling out of control. You don't have to follow the Twelve Step model, but if you'd like some steps, we offer twelve of our own for those who are willing to admit their lives are more than a little out of control:

TWELVE STEPS FOR THOSE WHOSE LIVES ARE OUT OF CONTROL

1. We admit we are powerless over busyness and technology and that our lives have become out of control as a result.
2. We have come to believe that a Power greater than ourselves (the ultimate community of One!) can restore us to sanity.
3. We have made a decision to turn our wills and our lives over to the care of the God revealed in Scripture.
4. We have taken a searching and fearless moral inventory of our priorities, our schedules, our use of technology, and our lack of community.

5. We have admitted to God, to ourselves, and to other human beings the exact nature of our out-of-control lifestyle.

6. We are entirely ready to have God remove all of these defects of character that underlie our need to remain busy and out of control.

7. We have humbly asked God to remove our shortcomings (including our excessive cell-phone usage).

8. We have made a list of all persons we have neglected and have become willing to make amends to all of them.

9. We have made direct amends to such persons wherever possible, except when to do so would injure them or others.

10. We have continued to take a personal inventory of our schedules, and when we have become overbooked or misplaced our priorities, we promptly admit it.

11. We have sought to incorporate the practices of Sabbath, solitude, and meditation, practicing the presence of God and praying for His peace, the knowledge of His will, and the power to carry that out.

12. Having had a spiritual awakening as a result of these steps, we have tried to carry this message to fellow out-of-control people and to practice these principles in all our affairs.

Your Place in Community

Once you begin to experience the benefits of getting your life in order, we believe you will want to share your positive experiences with others. You should! Certainly there are those in your church, your small group, or your extended family who might benefit from what you've learned. But we encourage you to think beyond the obvious. Maybe you are a part of a professional organization, community service group, neighborhood organization, running group, moms' support group, or educational group. These are part of your community as well. If you are open, you will have conversations that share these principles. None of us is immune to the effects of our culture, and all of us can use help in managing the pressures of time and technology.

By passing on what you've learned, you are receiving a double blessing. You've been helped, and you are able to help others. So why not "pay it forward" and let the blessing continue? As you share what you've learned, you are also reinforcing your commitment to keep practicing what you know. You're making yourself visible, and therefore accountable.

We believe in these principles. We're committed to living by them and helping others to do so. We'd like you to join us in that commitment, because there's collective power in community. Can you imagine a large and growing community of people committed to peace and simplicity, willing to do what it takes to secure and maintain them? Isn't that a great thought?

Listen, we haven't written this book to make you (or us, or anyone else) feel warm and fuzzy about doing less. We've written it so that you and others might actively engage the culture in change. We've seen the change in our own lives by putting these practices in place, and we've been blessed. We want you to experience what we have and to pass it on. God has called His people to be salt and light, but both salt and light need community to be fully appreciated. So find your place in the community of the called-out and committed. Get involved. Share the good news that we don't have to live fried, frazzled, and frantic lives just because everyone around us does.

Like Lance Armstrong, Mother Teresa, and David Rozelle, we need not only the desire, but the support to meet the challenge.

That's *your* place in community. So what do you say? Will you join us? The invitation stands.

WHAT IF . . .

. . . you actually allowed someone else to help you carry your burdens?

. . . you stopped being critical of others as an excuse to go it alone?

. . . you lived a life that truly impacted your supportive and local communities for the better?

YOUR NEW LIFE IN HIS CONTROL

*I wished to live deliberately, to front only the essential facts of life,
and see if I could not learn what it had to teach, and not, when
I came to die, discover that I had not lived.*
—HENRY DAVID THOREAU

Years ago, I found myself seated on a grassy hill in a gated community with my friend Charles. I have known Charles for many years, and we used to live in the same city. After some small talk, he peered over his pristine neighborhood and turned to me and said, "I love living here in Atlanta. The quality of life here is so much better than in Houston." Being from Houston, I did all I could to refrain from pushing "King Charles" off the hill, but, on the other hand, I knew exactly what he meant.

It wasn't really Houston versus Atlanta; he was talking about having a comfortable life: a nice, well-paying job, a nice house, a nice car, some nice clothes, a nice wife, some nice kids, a nice school, and nice vacations. No doubt about it, Charles had moved up the ladder of success and was now living a much better quality of life than he ever had in Houston. As far as the so-called American dream was concerned, Charles had it all. But what about those things money can't buy?

It's a sad truth that you can have all the luxuries this world has to offer and still not have peace of mind. Knowing Charles a little more deeply than perhaps some of his new Atlanta friends, I was aware of the fact that all these surface niceties only masked the pain he was experiencing due to a marriage relationship gone cold and disinterested children. It's great to have nice things—nothing wrong with that. But so often the high-speed pursuit of the American dream leaves our souls running on empty and yearning for the "missing peace."

Paul wrote to the Romans: "Therefore, having been justified by faith, we have peace with God through our Lord Jesus Christ" (5:1 NKJV). Peace in this life and peace in the life to come flow our way only through knowing, living, and trusting in Jesus Christ.

A while back I had the opportunity to spend several hours with Dr. Richard Pratt, a professor of Old Testament theology at Reformed Theological Seminary in Orlando, Florida. I had asked to meet with Dr. Pratt to talk about a book he had written many years before on apologetics. After discussing different critical theories concerning the Bible, the differences between modernity and postmodernity, and how many angels can tap dance on the top of a pinhead (just kidding), Dr. Pratt said something I was finally able to wrap my mind around: "What it really all boils down to is following Jesus. It's that simple. We have decided to follow Jesus Christ."

When you think about it, the professor is right. It *is* that simple. If we are in Christ, our lives should be all about following Him. And if we desire peace with God, it comes only through trusting and following the Prince of Peace.

LET'S GET FOCUSED

The out-of-control life has stifled our ability to connect with Christ and others in a meaningful way. This book is meant to encourage us all to stop the madness and say *no* to the hectic OOC lifestyle and *yes* to following Jesus. Every single one of the principles, practices, and movements we've mentioned finds its root in Christ: The Sabbath is about resting in Christ on that special day as well as in an overall attitude of the mind. Solitude is about withdrawing from the crazy pace of everyday life to be with Christ. Prayer and meditation are about getting the Word deep into our souls and acquiring the mind of Christ. Prioritizing and learning when to say yes and when to say no is about ordering our lives to be more effective for Christ. Moving away from technology and toward community is about finding abundant life and accountability in the body of Christ. All these practices and movements have meaning because they are tethered to Christ. Outside of Him they are merely rules. But when He is the End, they provide the means by which we truly abide in Him.

Now, perhaps you are saying to yourself, *Truly abiding in Christ sounds great, but I don't have the time or the energy to do all this stuff . . . I know I need to change, I need to pray more, I need to get my priorities in order, but I'm simply exhausted.* Maybe you feel as if all we have done is added to your to-do list. If that's where you are, let us free you up.

LET'S GET PRACTICAL

First of all, if you can digest this entire book with the practices and movements we are suggesting, great. Knock yourself out. If you find yourself feeling a bit more intimidated, relax. Simply start where you are. If you can apply just one or two of the concepts from this book, you'll be off to a great start.

You may say, "All I can do right now is try to carve out more time for solitude and prayer." Wonderful. Start there. You may say, "I can try to take a full day off and practice the Sabbath." Excellent. Maybe your first step is to join a local church and get plugged in to a community that will encourage you in your move away from the OOC life. The main thing is not to get overwhelmed. Trying to apply all the practices and movements right away could very well lead to failure (which often ends only in guilt and more frustration than you perhaps began with).

Remember, the disciples couldn't even watch and pray with Jesus for one hour in the Garden of Gethsemane. No doubt they were bold and courageous men who were genuinely attempting to follow Jesus, but they also had many failures and rough spots along the way. As with most things in life, you have to crawl before you can walk and walk before you can run.

We are not lowering the bar but simply being realistic as fellow sinners who are living in a sinful world. As you crawl, walk, or run, let what Christ has done for you be your motivator. If we've trusted Him for salvation, can we not trust Him to help us with the rest? He gives us the strength we need to rise above our culture and draw nearer to Him.

I love to go to the beach. Something magical and powerful drew me to the ocean as a kid and continues to draw me back as an adult. I remember playing in the Atlantic Ocean near Myrtle Beach, South Carolina, as a boy. I tried to bodysurf the waves into shore. On many occasions I started out right in front of the condo we were staying in and gradually drifted thirty to forty yards down the beach without even knowing it. The current was subtle, yet strong. I swiftly learned to keep a steady eye on home base and to swim against the current when it started to sweep me away. Sometimes I even had to get out of the water for a while and walk back.

Our out-of-control culture is like that current. It can slowly and stealthily take you places you don't want to go, and one day you'll wake up and realize how far you have drifted from everything that truly matters in life. The practices and power movements in this book serve as anchors in the midst of a culture that would keep us adrift and alone on a wide, wild sea. What will happen if you drop these anchors in your life?

What if you drop the anchor of the Sabbath? Every week you make the commitment to take a full day off of work in order to worship, reflect, and recharge your spiritual, physical, and emotional batteries. You will begin to see the grace of God in your life. You will learn to daily rest in all the many tangible and intangible blessings that flow your way because of who Christ is and what He has done. You will have set the tone for your week by engaging in a rhythm of work and rest. You will see the peace of God in your life.

What if you drop the anchor of solitude? Every day you set aside a time to get silent and still. You begin by breathing deeply and slowly in order to relax and focus on God's power to sustain you. You dive into study of the Word and prayer with a new vigor. You will begin to see God working with you in your relationships at work and at home. You will know that God's strength is with you as you walk through the tough and tedious moments of everyday living. You will gain God's perspective on the many events, both high and low, that you face from day to day. You will realize that you are not alone in your swim against the current—He is with you. You will have peace.

What if you drop the anchor of prayer? Every day you take the opportunities that come your way to communicate with God. Remember, communication involves listening, not just talking. During a five-minute coffee break at work or when you are in the car alone on the commute or on the way to pick up the kids, you find yourself stealing moments with God in prayer. You say no to picking up the cell phone to talk to others and instead try to connect with God. It may be as simple as, "Help" or "Thanks." You may use this moment to quote silently or aloud a verse of Scripture that you are meditating on in your times of solitude. What if you get joyfully serious about prayer? The peace of God that passes all comprehension will march around your heart. James said we have not because we ask not. Are you willing to start asking with a heart that truly seeks satisfaction in Him above all?

Testimonials

If you think it's impossible to fight the current and win, let us encourage you with some examples of people who *are* fighting and winning—people who have implemented some of these practices into their lives and are experiencing the kind of peace and rest only God can provide.

Jason Baker is a young, successful commercial real estate broker in Houston, Texas.

"Life is so busy that if my wife and I do not take the time to get away from the everyday pace at the beginning of each year and make it a point to listen to the Lord and to one another, we end up running around in circles feeling scattered and directionless, disconnected from each other and from God's deeper purposes for our lives and His kingdom. That's why each January, the two of us take a day or two to retreat with one another and with the Lord. We use this time to seek God's heart for the upcoming year and set goals in our individual lives and for our marriage. We cover everything from finances, to mission trips we want to take, to friendships we want to pursue. By the end of our time together, we not only have a good understanding of the direction the Lord wants us to head for the upcoming year, but we understand the desires and goals of each other's hearts. But it never fails—at the end of every year as we look back, we see that God has not only guided and directed us each step of the way, He has surpassed and exceeded any goal we ever could have made."

COLLYNN HARPER lives in Orlando, Florida, and is the chief executive officer and director of a household of five children.

"When my husband and I moved to Russia in 1992 with our one-year-old son, we were immediately forced into a life of simplicity. Entertainment consisted of gathering with others. There were no choices as to what we should do or where we should go, the only choice to be made was whose home would it be this time? Eating out was a rare treat and, in our early years there, required a drive to Finland to find a Western restaurant. Appointments were often scheduled with one person per day because an appointment usually consisted of a very long walk together and a talk that could last all afternoon.

"When we left there with three young children we asked ourselves how we could maintain a lifestyle where the things that really mattered would not get swept away. We also desired to keep the things in life that should be 'treats' as treats rather than have them become things we felt we were entitled to. This began for us with small choices like living in Orlando yet not having passes to Disney that would enable us to go whenever we liked, instead reserving that privilege for the most special occasions.

"In bigger ways, our commitment to try to maintain simplicity has evolved over the years. It is like trying to stop a speeding train, but we have found once we put forth the effort and fight through the resistance, we have a richer, fuller life to be enjoyed. One recent example has been our experience of having long dinner hours with our five children. They moan when they see us setting the big table, but once we get there, they laugh, tell stories, and enjoy one another in new ways. We have discovered it is a lot of small choices like these that lead to changed attitudes and a restful place to enjoy the life abundant God offers us."

RUSSELL DAVIS is a husband and father of three living in Austin, Texas.

"As I have moved well into my 40s, time seems to be shrinking as the demands on it expand. With a lovely wife who works outside the home, three young daughters, a demanding job, and church responsibilities, I've found that quality time as a family has become a valuable commodity. My wife and I are doing all we can to try and maintain balance and order. We haven't arrived yet, but over the past year or so we have begun taking steps toward controlling our time so that it does not control us.

"One step has been limiting the number of activities our children are involved in outside the home. Another step has been having dinner together as a family on a regular basis, which has allowed us to talk about our day and simply stay in touch with one another. A more recent step has been striving to make Sunday a true day of rest. On most Sundays, we leave the TV and radio off, have rest or nap time on Sunday afternoon, try not to go anywhere if we don't have to, and usually spend that time together as a family. While most of our days are committed to the ordinary necessities of living, we view Sunday as a day to relax and reflect, and we pray that God would grant us wisdom in the use of our discretionary time before it runs out."

KATHRIN MILBURY is a young single originally from Bavaria, Germany, who moved to the United States in her teens. She is currently a doctoral candidate in the Department of Psychology at the University of Houston.

"Three years ago, I read a book on purifying the mind. As a response, I substantially curtailed watching TV and reading magazines. Instead of watching some morning show, I committed this time to praying and studying the Bible. Initially, this time of quietness and reflection was just something else to do in my busy schedule. Gradually, as I became familiar with the Lord's gentle voice, I started to enjoy spending time with Him. Now, it totally amazes me when I think that the Lord God Almighty, my Creator and Savior, waits for me to spend quality time with Him.

"How could I possibly not find the time? How could spending time in His presence be something else to do? TV is such a time-wasting, excruciating bore in comparison. Additionally, the more He teaches me about Truth, the more annoyed I become with the media perpetuating mostly lies. Consequently, I have almost completely eliminated TV and magazines from my life—not as a sacrifice, but simply because I don't like them anymore. Reallocating media-time to Christ-time has tremendously changed my walk with the Lord."

Brig Jones is a consultant and Church Evangelism Director in St. Louis, Missouri.

"As a forty-one-year-old single man, I have learned that achieving maximum effectiveness in life is dependent on faith in Jesus Christ and the ability to maintain physical, emotional, and spiritual balance. However, accomplishing a healthy level of balance in this opportunistic and demanding world is a bit challenging. While my body desires strenuous and fatigue-inducing exercise, and my mind craves developing work-related strategies, and my soul longs for frequent and exciting social interaction, my person (as a whole) requires relaxation, decompression, and spiritual refueling. Therefore, it is imperative for me, even without the responsibilities of caring for a family, to be intentional and protective with my time in order to balance these needs.

"The activity which balances and refreshes me most is the study of God's Word and the prayerful and meditative interaction with the Lord Jesus Christ. My preferred times for this activity are in the morning, and then once again in the evening before I go to bed. My morning routine is to stop at my favorite coffee shop before I go to the office. I will sit by myself, read, and carefully study the Bible—underlining special or applicable passages—while I slowly drink my 'Americano.' I will typically spend anywhere from thirty minutes to an hour focusing on one to two chapters of God's Word and reflecting on His power, greatness, and love for me through Jesus Christ. I find this time tremendously necessary and invigorating. I do the same thing again at night, with more of an emphasis on prayer.

"This spiritual refreshment balances me and enables me to be more effective and content. Certainly, I experience tremendous joy and fulfillment from my friends, my family, good meals, movies, golf, and other hobbies. But without a doubt, it is the Lord, His Word, and His wonderful promise that the future blessings in heaven infinitely surpass the greatest blessings this world could offer, which keep me most energized, balanced, and happy."

DOUGAL CAMERON is the president and owner of Cameron Management, Inc., a commercial real estate company based in Houston and San Antonio, Texas.

"In 1998, our family of six (my wife and I have three boys, ages twelve, ten, and six, and one girl, age eleven), could not find enough time for regular family dinners together. So after much thought and prayer, we moved in the summer of 2000 to Chappell Hill, Texas (63 miles from Houston). I commute to the office, leaving at 5 AM and returning at 4 PM every day. We have family dinner together almost every evening. Also, we blew up the television (only family-gathering DVDs allowed). As a result, my daughter wasn't very happy with me for two years. She is over that now.

"My children did not understand what all the fuss was about and will not until they are thirty. But my wife and I are closer in our marriage, and our family knows how to enjoy each other. We hope to have a hospitality ministry as the kids leave for college that helps others who need to spiritually recharge, reboot, or renew."

LAUREN AND NATHAN BENESH are young newlyweds who live in Cambridge, Massachusetts. Nathan is working on a Ph.D. in geophysics at Harvard University, and Lauren is an administrative assistant to a number of deans there.

"My husband and I recently moved from a large city in Texas, where people would never consider walking across the street when they can drive, to Cambridge, MA, where people are encouraged to walk to their destinations. At first I doubted I would find walking everywhere an attribute of my new lifestyle; the convenience of driving simply cannot bear such a comparison, or so I thought. But, in hindsight, I think my favorite part of the move has been the change in our commutes.

"I have found that the ten-minute walk to my office at Harvard is immensely more tranquil than sitting in traffic. I am also much more aware of nature when I walk, even though my meanderings take place solely in the city. For example, I had a favorite tree to walk past in the autumn, when the leaves started changing color. I secretly called it my 'torch tree'—the leaves were so bright they were almost the color of fire—and every day when I passed it I welled up with thankfulness to God for His marvelous creation and artistry. And even if there are other pedestrians around, walking is usually a solitary activity; there is no radio to prove a distraction from my thoughts, for example.

"The few minutes I have to myself to spend quietly in my own mind has proved a valuable part of my morning. Another practice my husband and I have found helpful in preserving serenity in the midst of our busy schedules is muting the TV whenever the programming goes to commercials. Growing up, I saw my parents and grandparents do this, and I don't think I even found out other people didn't until I went to college. Nathan and I are not as consistent with muting every commercial as my family is, but we have found value in it whenever we have done it, especially after a particularly harried day. The absence of noise during that time helps foster an element of peace in our home."

NIKI PELLEGRIN is a young single who has a passion for seeing students grow in their relationship with Christ. She served on the youth staff of a church for a number of years, and she is currently a missionary with Leadertreks, a Chicago-based organization whose sole purpose is developing and equipping leaders to spread the Gospel. When on staff with the church, she regularly took part in what they called a "Day with the Lord."

"Our Day with the Lord was a time for us as a youth staff to get away from the crazy pace that often comes with working in a youth office. Once a month, this day was a nonnegotiable in our schedules. Its purpose was to seek rest and rejuvenation and to fill ourselves with God's Word. We always went away to a solitary place and stayed out there the length of a typical work day. Once we got to our location we would separate. We always wanted to make sure that it wasn't just a day with our books, but truly a day with the Lord. We turned off all cell phones, iPods, and wouldn't even talk to one another the whole time—it was just us, individually, and God. Then at the end of the day, we would come together and eat and discuss what God had revealed to each of us and make goals based on any revelations. I always left feeling more excited about God's Word and more equipped to pour into students' lives."

RENE WILLIS is a full-time homemaker who lives in Austin, Texas.

"Last year, my husband and I felt very overwhelmed with financial burdens and too many activities for the kids. Our lives were truly 'out of control,' and we knew that something had to change. Our home was not close to the school, and we found ourselves spending several hours a day driving to and from school. Precious time was spent in the car driving to all the various after-school activities and programs as well. After much prayer, personal retreats, and a lot of discussion around our priorities, we decided to 'downsize' by selling our home, reducing some expenses, and moving closer to the school. We also made the decision to limit the children's activities, and now we have much more time as a family. We have 'gained' several hours per day now because of this decision. Life isn't perfect, but we feel as if God has blessed our decision to simplify, and our quality time together as a family has been enhanced."

JAMES M. TOUR is the Chao Professor of Chemistry, Professor of Computer Science, and Professor of Mechanical Engineering and Materials Science in Rice University's Center for Nanoscale Science and Technology. He has about 215 scientific publications as well as numerous patents. He is also a cofounder and board member of Molecular Electronics Corp. He and his wife, Shireen, have four children—two daughters and two sons.

"About fifteen years ago, my beloved father-in-law, a faithful man who fears God, took me aside and suggested that I meet every morning with my family for the study of the Bible. Although I was the father of two small daughters, he told me that the years would quickly pass. As their father, I should be speaking scriptural truths daily into their lives in the time when they are young and moldable. It was the best advice I ever got.

"Even though I had been meeting with them daily to pray at mealtime and their bedtime, I had to define a set time for the systematic study and meditation on the Scriptures. That practice has yielded a bounty of fruit one-hundred-fold (Psalm 112:1–2). I even took our newborns (sometimes to my wife's dismay) from their cribs each morning to join us. My children know only of our daily rising at 5:30 AM to meet together as a family for study and prayer, and they look forward to it. After we study God's Word, we all get on our knees and pray, one by one. I close by placing my hand on each of their heads and praying a specific prayer for them for that day and for their future marriages and careers. By 6:00 AM, I am leaving the house for work.

"I recently asked my two daughters, ages eighteen and fifteen, what their fondest memories are regarding our family. Their responses were revealing. It was not our family vacations. It was not the games we had played together. It was not our family holidays together. Both daughters agreed, without a second thought, that the highlight of their growing up in the Tour family was our daily family prayer times!"

LET'S GET PERSONAL (YOUR STORY)

Crashing waves of worry pound against the shore of your mind as you sit beached in rush-hour traffic. You pick up your Blueberry Semi Mega Organizer 2008 and notice that you have 116 appointments tomorrow starting at 4:00 AM and ending at 9:00 PM. After the nine o'clock, you have to catch a 9:15 flight to New York. How are you going to squeeze in your 3.2 minutes of quality time with your mate, much less the 1.5 minutes of real time with your 2.5 kids, and still make that 9:15 flight to the Big Apple?

You mentally kick yourself in the rear for not shelling out an extra twelve hundred dollars to upgrade to the Blueberry Mega Organizer 2010. This little gem organizes your e-mail based on your priorities and has the best cell coverage on the planet, as well as a built-in fax machine, high-speed Internet access, 432 satellite TV stations, and a cappuccino maker all in one device that is small enough to fit into your pocket. You make a vow to buy this time-saving gadget after you return from your trip.

Suddenly, your Blueberry Semi Mega whatchamacallit blasts in your ear like an alarm clock, screaming at you to get out of bed and get moving. Wait a minute. This is your alarm clock, and it is 6:00 AM. It was just a nightmare . . . another hangover from the out-of-control life you once lived.

Before your feet touch the floor, you close your eyes for a few moments and thank God for another day to live fully and freely. After your brief prayer of thanks, you silently quote the twenty-third Psalm and embark on a new day. Yes, today will be another day filled with meetings, activities, events, and deadlines, but something has changed deep within. Though you still feel the burden of living in this out-of-control culture, you are not out of control. Having gained a better perspective on what really matters in life, you feel a new sense of faith and a deep trust in God as you face the challenges of a potentially chaotic day.

It's been three steady months of recovery from your old way of life with its overscheduling, its overindulging in activities, techno-toys, and a constant need for distraction. By implementing a consistent Sabbath day devoted to worship, reflection, and rejuvenation, you have set the tone for the rest of your week. Instead of seeing it as a wasted day or a grueling time of personal sacrifice, you now actually look forward to it and see it as a blessing that you'll want to maintain and protect for as long as you live.

Your times of solitude and prayer throughout the course of your day have allowed you to see God work in even the seemingly mundane and ordinary events of life. Sure, you have moments, even days, of lapsing back into the old OOC lifestyle, but you have learned to address the lies that are at the root of these moments and take them captive before they have time to send you on that downward spiral to physical, mental, and spiritual exhaustion.

This is our prayer for you. May God grant you His peace and rest as you seek Him in all you do.

WHAT IF . . .

. . . you tried to implement just one of these practices today?

. . . you dropped the anchor of the Sabbath and experienced the rest of God in a new and profound way?

. . . you didn't simply let this book and God's truth about peace, rest, and simplicity merely enlighten you but you actually let it change your life?

STUDY GUIDE

CHAPTER 1: A CULTURE SPINNING OUT OF CONTROL

1. In what ways do you feel "out of control" in your life?

2. Make a list of all your worries/concerns/stressors.

3. In what ways, if any, do you find yourself seeking approval from those around you? Even from God?

4. Read Galatians 3:1–3. How does this passage relate to the grind of seeking approval from others?

5. In what ways do you feel overloaded with information?

6. In what ways, if any, have you found that your ultra-accessibility has actually made you less accessible for the relationships and practices that matter most?

7. Reflect on Matthew 14:23 and Luke 5:15–16. What *did* Jesus do?

8. Ask God to give you the proper perspective as you read this book and as you take an inventory of your own life, and pray that He would reveal to you whatever else you need to lay at His feet along the way.

Chapter 2: Are *You* Out of Control?

1. Grade yourself in the following areas. It may help you to go back to the chapter and review each category.
   (Rate yourself on a scale of 1–10, 10 being the most healthy.)

   _____ Out of shape (physical symptoms)
   _____ Well rested
   _____ Regular exercise
   _____ Eating healthy
   _____ Caffeine intake
   _____ Lack of general aches and pains that may be warning signs
   _____ Out of sorts (emotional/mental symptoms)
   _____ Out of touch (relational symptoms)

List the people that matter most in your life. Evaluate how you are doing at staying connected with each of them. Do you know their greatest source of joy, hope, and anxiety right now?

Grade   Name

_____   _____

_____   _____

_____   _____

_____   _____

_____   _____

_____   _____

_____   _____

Continue grading yourself in the following areas:

_____ Out of time (scheduling symptoms)

_____ Out of focus (perspective symptoms)

_____ Out of balance (interpersonal symptoms)

_____ Out of order (spiritual symptoms)

2. After rating yourself in these overall areas, keep your results in mind as you see opportunities to make improvements. What is your area with the greatest opportunity for improvement?

3. Read Luke 2:52. How does this simple yet profound verse relate to your need for balance?

4. Discuss how Isaiah 44:6–8 and Psalm 95:3–5 both show who is really in control.

CHAPTER 3: SEVEN LIES THAT FEED THE OOC LIFESTYLE

1. Why must we "think right" before we can "do right"?

2. Read Proverbs 23:7; 2 Corinthians 10:5; and Romans 12:1–2. What do these verses tell us about "right thinking"?

3. What is the difference between having peace with God and having the peace of God?

4. What does Matthew 6:25–34 have to say about our worth in God's eyes?

5. Why is resting so necessary that even Jesus did it?

6. Why should we live as though we're about to die?

7. Take Jon Foreman's quote and replace his words with words of your own in the given blank: "It was a beautiful letdown the day I knew all the _____

_____

_____ this world had to offer me would never do."

8. Reflect on James 4:13–17. What is "the good" God is telling us to focus on?

Chapter 4: It All Starts with the Sabbath

1. *Before* reading this chapter, what were your perceptions about the Sabbath?

2. *After* reading this chapter, what do you see as the primary benefits of Sabbath rest? Which of these is your greatest area of need?

3. Study Exodus 20:1–19 carefully and prayerfully. Why do we virtually ignore commandment number 4?

4. Read Genesis 2:1–2. Why do you think God made man and woman on the sixth day?

5. Study Mark 2:27 and Matthew 12:8. How did Jesus recast the Sabbath?

6. Write out a starting point for beginning to practice some type of Sabbath rest. Choose even a small period of time to set aside each week to get into the habit. You may need to start with just one hour per week and then gradually work up to a Sabbath day. The goal here is to get in the mind-set and get started.

CHAPTER 5: THE PRACTICE OF SOLITUDE AND SILENCE

1. Read Mark 1:35 and Luke 4:42.

2. Make a personal assessment of your time alone. How much time during the week do you currently take to step away in solitude and silence?

3. This chapter gave three reasons why we take time for solitude. Discuss the seemingly paradoxical idea that taking time for solitude works to benefit our relationships in community.

4. After reading this chapter, if you are making a decision to become intentional about starting or increasing your time spent in solitude and silence, then plan for it today. When planning, consider how much time you spend in silence right now and be realistic in starting with a reasonable goal to build on in time. Also keep in mind your makeup as an introvert or extrovert when setting a goal. Make time for it—choose a time of day that you can consistently keep.

5. Make a place for it. Designate a place that will be your regular place of solitude.

CHAPTER 6: THE PRACTICE OF PRESENCE

1. Look up and "meditate" on these verses about meditation: Psalm 63:6–7; Genesis 24:63; Psalm 119:97–101; Philippians 4:8.

2. Why do we shy away from prayer?

3. Differentiate between Christian meditation and New Age meditation with regard to detaching and attaching.

4. Try incorporating some of the Short Prayers and Prayer Practices at the end of the chapter into your personal time as you pursue practicing the presence of God. You may want to write them down in the space below.

5. Look up Matthew 26:41 (NKJV). What did Jesus mean by the statement "The spirit . . . is willing, but the flesh is weak"?

6. Reflect on Ephesians 6:18. How can you incorporate this verse into your everyday life?

Chapter 7: Move Your Priorities

1. Make a quick list of what is truly most important to you.

2. Now take a moment to evaluate your priorities and worldview only by how you spend your time and your money. If you were an outsider looking in at your own life, what would you conclude your priorities to be, based on these two indicators?

3. Now that we know where you are spending your time, let's get more detailed. Write down all of your activities, responsibilities, and commitments for a week. Now rank or sort them into three categories: essential, nonessential, and trivial. Do they reflect your priorities?

<u>Essential</u>   <u>Nonessential</u>   <u>Trivial</u>

4. Read Isaiah 55:2. Contrast the things that satisfy with the things that don't.

5. Look up Psalm 27:4 and Numbers 18:29. How can you make these passages a reality in your life?

6. In order to start practicing contentment, make a list of some of the things you are thankful for this week.

7. Looking back at the section on "The Power of One"—can you remember a critical moment or experience that brought your life priorities into crystal clear perspective?

8. Looking at your stated priorities in exercise #1 and then your schedule and checkbook in exercises #2 and #3 above, where would be a good place to start saying no and setting some boundaries?

9. Read Matthew 6:33–34. What does "seeking the kingdom" look like in your everyday life?

10. How does "seeking the kingdom first" eliminate worry?

CHAPTER 8: MOVE AWAY FROM TECHNOLOGY

1. It is easy to recognize the benefits and conveniences of modern technology; can you now identify some of the drawbacks? Can you be specific about how it may have negatively impacted your own life?

2. Evaluate and list some of the ways that technology is controlling you rather than you controlling it.

3. Discuss how 1 Corinthians 6:12 and 2 Peter 2:19 relate to the issue of technology.

4. Read Genesis 11:1–9. How does the Tower of Babel account compare to modern technology?

5. List some ways you can reverse the curse of technology and take control of it in order to let it work for you.

6. Look up Galatians 4:9 and Galatians 5:1. How should we view excessive uses of technology in light of these verses?

CHAPTER 9: MOVE INTO COMMUNITY

1. First, define what we are referring to in the three levels of community. Then, evaluate your life and ask yourself the questions that follow to see if you are tapped into the power of each of these essential communities.

   The Ultimate Community: _____

   The Local Community: _____

   A Supportive Community: _____

2. Do you know and trust in the God of the Ultimate Trinity? When we even begin to understand the very deep and complex nature of the Trinity as the ultimate community, it becomes a model for our own lives. How is each of us wired to reflect the Trinity in our relationships?

3. Are you an active and necessary part of a local community? Which of the following best describes your connection to a local church?

Completely disconnected—Don't even know where to find a local church.

Flirting with connection—Church-hop to various congregations but haven't committed to becoming a member or to serving in one church loyally.

Regular attendee—Go to one church fairly regularly or regularly but either haven't joined or am not plugged in to the true life and service of the church.

Nonparticipating member—Regular attendee and member but do not serve in a vital capacity.

Active member—Have officially joined the church membership and have an essential role in the church that would be missed if I wasn't there.

4. Read Acts 2:42 and 1 John 1:7. What does it mean to have true fellowship?

5. Define your supportive community. If you can't easily define this, stop here and identify some individual people that could potentially function as your supportive community.

6. What are some ways that your supportive community can "be on the same page" as you about reordering your life? Is there anyone you would like to join you on this mission?

7. Read Galatians 6:2 and Romans 12:10. From a practical standpoint, how can you carry someone's burdens?

CONCLUSION: YOUR NEW LIFE IN HIS CONTROL

1. How do the practices and movements in this book find their root in Christ?

2. What will happen if you "drop the anchor" of the Sabbath? . . . prayer? . . . solitude?

3. If your life has changed since you have implemented some of the practices in this book, tell your story to the group or write it out in the space below.

4. Study Philippians 4:4–9. Turn this passage into a prayer and meditate on it in your time alone with God.

About the Authors

Ben Young, M.Div., leads seminars on how to build success-ful dating and marriage relationships. Ben is a teaching pastor at the 40,000-member Second Baptist Church in Houston, Texas.

Samuel Adams, Psy.D., is a licensed psychologist. He earned his master's from Western Seminary and a doctorate from George Fox University. He maintains a full-time counseling practice in Austin, Texas.

www.YoungandAdams.org

Also visit The Center for Personal Peace
at www.Center4Peace.com

ACKNOWLEDGMENTS

Our deepest thanks and love go to Elliott and Julie, our beautiful and godly wives. Your sacrifice and support made this book a reality. Thank you for always being there and for living out the grace of God in our families.

To Sarah Welch and Toni Richmond for your tireless energy, input, and effort that you gave to this project.

A special thanks goes to Leigh McLeroy, who made this book flow smoothly in so many ways. Thanks for your hard work, insights, and willingness to go the second mile.

We also want to thank Brian Hampton, Kyle Olund, and Jonathan Merkh at Thomas Nelson Publishers for catching the vision of this project from the get-go and seeing it through until the end.

To Rabbi Yaakov Lipsky, Richard Foster, Henri Nouwen, and Abraham Joshua Heschel for living out many of these practices in the real world and inspiring countless others to do the same.

All honor, praise, and glory to the Father, Son, and the Holy Spirit, who call us to experience an everlasting peace.

THE TEN COMMANDMENTS OF DATING

Are you tired of pouring time, energy and money into relationships that start off great and end with heartache? If so, you need *The Ten Commandments of Dating* to give you the hard-hitting, black-and-white, practical guidelines that will address your questions and frustrations about dating.

ISBN: 0-7852-7022-1

THE TEN COMMANDMENTS OF DATING STUDENT EDITION

The 10 Commandments of Dating, Student Edition provides you with ten time-tested relationship laws that protect you from the pitfalls of modern dating and will help you practice good relationship habits for the future. This book gives you practical, no-nonsense advice on how to build positive relationships with the opposite sex and avoid all the heartache and regret. If you keep the ten commandments, you will be on the road to making wise dating decisions!

ISBN: 0-7852-6059-5

THE ONE: A REALISTIC GUIDE TO CHOOSING YOUR SOUL MATE

In their bestselling book, *The Ten Commandments of Dating*, Ben Young and Samuel Adams showed singles how to date effectively. Now *The One* shows Christians who to date and how to negotiate the difficulties of choosing a soul mate.

ISBN: 0-7852-6744-1

DEVOTIONS FOR DATING COUPLES

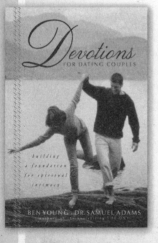

Authors Ben Young and Sam Adams offer this unique devotional for dating couples as a companion to their books *The Ten Commandments of Dating* and *The One*.

ISBN: 0-7852-6749-2